Is Jesus God?

God in the Flesh: Jesus' Divine Identity

Is Jesus God?

God in the Flesh: Jesus' Divine Identity

Vinu V Das

TP
Tabor Press

ISBN 978-1-997541-00-4

Table of Contents

Chapter 1: Introducing the Central Question

1.1 Why the Question Matters

Few questions in the realm of Christian theology generate as much intrigue, scrutiny, and debate as the one at the heart of this book: **Is Jesus God?** Throughout the centuries, believers and skeptics alike have wrestled with the identity of Jesus Christ, sometimes with profound consequences for how they worship, how they understand salvation, and how they live out their faith. From the earliest days of Christianity, followers have insisted that the identity of Jesus is not merely a peripheral issue but the very cornerstone on which the Church is built (Ephesians 2:19–20). Jesus's question to his disciples—"Who do you say that I am?" (Matthew 16:15)—still echoes in the hearts and minds of Christians and non-Christians today. Thus, while other theological issues can be of secondary importance, the claim that Jesus is fully divine remains decisive for

Christian self-understanding, shaping its doctrines of salvation, worship, and the nature of God.

The Significance for Christian Worship and Devotion

One of the primary reasons this question matters is its impact on the nature and focus of **Christian worship**. If Jesus truly is God, then worship directed to Him is both appropriate and mandatory from a Christian point of view. Prayer, praise, and adoration—traditionally offered to God alone—would rightly be directed toward Jesus (Philippians 2:9–11). Conversely, if Jesus were *not* God, then worshiping Him would be both theologically incorrect and ethically problematic (Exodus 20:3). Hence, the divinity of Christ undergirds the very essence of Christian worship practices and shapes the liturgical life of churches worldwide.

Historical traditions, including those of the **early Church Fathers**, tie the question of Jesus' identity closely to the liturgical expressions of the earliest Christian communities (Kelly, *Early Christian Doctrines*, 1978). Textual evidence suggests that the earliest followers of Jesus sang hymns that acknowledged Jesus' lordship and divine attributes (Philippians 2:5–11), a practice that implicitly sets Jesus apart from mere human teachers or prophets. Thus, the matter of whether Jesus is God is not an abstract theological proposition but a practical reality that touches upon the daily spiritual life of believers.

Implications for the Doctrine of Salvation

Just as significant is how this central question informs the **doctrine of salvation**. If Jesus is God incarnate, the incarnation, crucifixion, and resurrection carry a unique and absolute weight. In Christian teaching, salvation hinges on the belief that God Himself intervened in human history to redeem humanity (2 Corinthians 5:19). The union of divine and human natures in Jesus would mean that Christ's sacrifice is *capable* of atoning for the sins of the world, bridging an otherwise impossible chasm between a holy God and fallen humanity (Stott, *The Cross of Christ*, 1986).

On the other hand, if Jesus were merely a highly exalted man or prophet, Christian soteriology (the theology of salvation) would be radically different. The question would then arise: *How can a mere human fully reconcile humanity with the infinite, transcendent Creator?* Or, conversely, is such reconciliation even necessary in the same sense? The entire understanding of grace, atonement, and divine mercy would shift dramatically. Thus, at the heart of Christian preaching—which proclaims that Christ died for our sins (1 Corinthians 15:3) and rose again (1 Corinthians 15:4)—lies the premise that only God could accomplish such a rescue plan.

Shaping Christian Ethics and Mission

Beyond worship and soteriology, the conviction that Jesus is God or is not God reshapes an individual's **ethical framework** and sense of **mission**. If Jesus embodies the very character of God in human form (Hebrews 1:3), then His teachings about love, forgiveness, humility, and self-sacrifice are not just wise suggestions from a profound moral teacher. They become direct revelations of God's will and character for humanity—teachings that should be obeyed with devotion and reverence. For many Christians, modeling one's life after Jesus is not purely a matter of admiring a historical figure, but of attempting to mirror the very nature of God in everyday conduct.

Similarly, **Christian mission**—the Church's mandate to share the gospel and serve the world—stems from Jesus' final instructions (Matthew 28:18–20). If Jesus is understood as divine, His words carry the weight of God's own command. As such, evangelism and discipleship become not merely institutional expansions but spiritual imperatives grounded in divine authority. This theological underpinning impels believers across centuries and continents to invest in missionary endeavors, charitable works, and community development efforts, seeking to demonstrate and proclaim God's love as manifested in Christ.

1.2 Jesus in the Modern Conversation

The question of Jesus' divinity continues to resonate in the **modern religious and cultural landscape**, though it has taken on new shapes under the pressures of contemporary scholarship, pluralism, media influences, and global communication. Today, one can explore a vast array of opinions about Jesus with just a few keystrokes online. Debates that once occurred in scholarly journals now unfold instantly across social media. This hyper-connected environment makes it vital to carefully discern reliable sources and to understand how modern perspectives on Jesus arise, whether from academic research, popular culture, or various religious traditions.

Scholarly Debates and Popular-Level Curiosity

A key aspect of the modern conversation involves **New Testament scholarship**, which rigorously examines biblical texts for historical and literary authenticity. Scholars such as Bart D. Ehrman, N. T. Wright, and Richard Bauckham have contributed significantly to contemporary discussions about how the early Church viewed Jesus and whether those views align with the belief in His divinity (Ehrman, *How Jesus Became God*, 2014; Bauckham, *Jesus and the Eyewitnesses*, 2006). Though these scholars differ in their conclusions, their research underscores the complexity of exploring Jesus' identity through the lens of history, textual criticism, and theology.

At a popular level, authors like Lee Strobel (*The Case for Christ*, 1998) have attempted to translate scholarly arguments into more accessible formats, appealing to those who seek answers but may not be versed in academic theology. With the rise of documentaries, podcasts, and blogs, interest in Jesus' identity no longer stays confined to seminarians or pastors; it becomes part of a broader cultural discourse.

Influence of Pluralism and Postmodernity

Another dimension of the modern conversation is shaped by **religious pluralism** and **postmodern thought**. Pluralistic societies celebrate a tapestry of beliefs and traditions, often placing them on equal footing. In this environment, the exclusive claim that Jesus is God can be met with discomfort or resistance. Many argue that asserting Jesus as God is too narrow, potentially undermining the legitimacy of other faith traditions. Thus, Christian apologists are often called to engage thoughtfully and humbly, demonstrating that claiming Jesus' divinity need not equate to disrespecting other religions.

From a **postmodern** vantage point, objective truth claims are frequently received with suspicion. Some argue that any declaration of divine identity is socially constructed or influenced by power dynamics within religious communities (Lyotard, *The Postmodern Condition*, 1979). The postmodern mindset challenges Christians to present not only historical evidence or traditional teachings but also to exhibit the transformational authenticity that faith in a divine Jesus can bring to personal and communal life. People are often drawn not just by the claim of Jesus' divinity but by seeing how belief in that divinity fosters selflessness, compassion, and justice in tangible ways.

Media Portrayals and Public Perception

Whether through movies, TV specials, or viral internet articles, **media portrayals** of Jesus profoundly influence public perception. Some films and documentaries present Jesus as a wandering teacher, emphasizing His humanity at the expense of His divinity. Others depict Him in a highly reverential, almost otherworldly manner. The tension between these portrayals can confuse those who are unfamiliar with biblical scholarship or the nuances of Christian tradition. Moreover, sensational headlines that question Jesus' existence or identity tend to draw attention, even when the

11

underlying claims might be tenuous upon closer inspection (Evans, *Fabricating Jesus*, 2006).

Challenges and Opportunities for the Church

For churches today, the ongoing conversation about Jesus' divinity presents both **challenges and opportunities**. On the one hand, skepticism is more visible than ever, and believers can feel pressure to water down or re-interpret central doctrines to fit in with prevailing cultural sentiments. On the other hand, never before has the Church had so many resources to engage questions about Jesus in an informed manner. Digital libraries, online sermons, and global Christian communities can equip believers to articulate with greater clarity why they uphold the historical Christian position on Jesus as God.

Moreover, the Church can use the contemporary hunger for authentic spirituality as an avenue for apologetics and evangelism. While intellectual arguments remain valuable, many individuals are persuaded by how Christian communities *embody* Christ's love and demonstrate a distinctive ethic that they believe originates in Jesus' divine nature (John 13:34–35). This combination of reasoned explanation and visible compassion can speak powerfully in a fragmented world searching for hope and meaning.

1.3 A Roadmap for Investigation

With the **significance** of the question "Is Jesus God?" established and its **modern context** surveyed, this section is to clarify **how** this book intends to approach the subject. Given the multifaceted nature of Christology—biblical, historical, theological, philosophical—this investigation will require a coherent method and a respectful dialogue with diverse perspectives.

Rationale for the Method

Any thorough examination of Jesus' divinity necessarily spans several domains of inquiry:

1. **Biblical Exegesis and Canonical Context** – Because the Bible remains the primary source for Christian claims about Jesus, a careful reading of both Old and New Testament texts is indispensable. While later chapters will delve more deeply into the key passages, our roadmap begins by acknowledging the centrality of Scripture to the Christian faith (2 Timothy 3:16).

2. **Historical and Cultural Background** – Understanding the first-century Jewish and Greco-Roman milieu sheds light on how Jesus' contemporaries might have perceived Him. A claim to deity would have had distinct implications within a staunchly monotheistic Jewish context or a pluralistic pagan culture.

3. **Theological and Philosophical Reflection** – Even once biblical texts and historical contexts are explored, one must consider how the concept of *deity* itself is understood. Philosophical and theological debates about the nature of God, the interplay between the human and the divine, and the limits of human language all come to bear on how one interprets biblical statements about Jesus.

4. **Church History and Ecumenical Councils** – Although the earliest Christians certainly held strong beliefs regarding Jesus' divine identity, the precise language used to articulate His two natures—fully God and fully human—was shaped by centuries of doctrinal reflection. Later chapters will trace these developments without duplicating the foundational discussion we have here.

5. **Practical and Devotional Dimensions** – An integrated approach to Christology recognizes that doctrine is not merely a theoretical exercise; it impacts personal devotion and community life. The assertion that Jesus is God invites worship, prayer, and ethical transformation in ways that a purely human Jesus would not.

Balancing Depth and Accessibility

A second element of this roadmap involves **balancing depth and accessibility**. On one hand, the question "Is Jesus God?" deserves serious academic attention. On the other hand, a purely academic discourse might be inaccessible for many believers or seekers who approach the topic out of spiritual curiosity or a desire to deepen their personal faith. Therefore, the content will aim to be **informative** without being unnecessarily technical, incorporating references to major scholars, councils, and theological viewpoints, while simultaneously providing clear explanations and practical reflections.

Encouraging Dialogue and Reflection

A final key component of this roadmap is **dialogue**. Rather than seeking to impose a dogmatic conclusion, this book aspires to present the rich tapestry of evidence and reflection that supports the Christian claim that Jesus is God. The hope is to foster a space where readers can critically engage with the arguments, weigh alternative perspectives, and arrive at informed convictions about who Jesus is. Throughout the journey, discussion questions, points for reflection, or brief sidebars may appear (especially in subsequent chapters), inviting deeper thought and community-based exploration (Grenz, *Theology for the Community of God*, 1994).

In this spirit, the roadmap also acknowledges that some readers may come from non-Christian or multi-faith backgrounds and might hold different assumptions about scripture, tradition, or spiritual experiences. Rather than dismiss those viewpoints, this book considers them worth engaging, treating them not as obstacles but as opportunities to clarify why historic Christian teaching insists on Jesus' divine identity.

Chapter 2: Historical and Cultural Backdrop

2.1 First-Century Judea

The Geography and Political Setting

First-century Judea was a relatively small region in the eastern Mediterranean, yet it occupied a strategic position at the crossroads of Africa, Asia, and Europe. Governed by Rome since 63 BC, Judea was officially brought under Roman rule when General Pompey intervened in a power dispute among local Jewish leaders (Sanders, *Judaism: Practice and Belief*, 1992). By the time of Jesus' ministry, the political climate had become a patchwork of direct Roman governance in some territories and rule by client kings (like the Herodian dynasty) in others. This mixture of imperial oversight and local monarchy provided a complicated setting where Jewish religious authorities often had to negotiate with Roman officials to maintain their own leadership roles.

The day-to-day governance of Judea involved a series of **Roman prefects** or procurators, the most famous of whom was Pontius Pilate (AD 26–36). Pilate's rule coincided with Jesus' public ministry and eventual crucifixion. His authority was considerable, including the power to appoint the high priest and to oversee criminal prosecutions for capital crimes, but his position depended upon keeping Judea peaceful and fiscally productive for Rome. Any signs of rebellion or civil unrest were taken seriously and could result in severe punishments (Josephus, *Antiquities of the Jews*, Book 18).

Religious Factions and Sects

1. **Pharisees** Among the most influential religious parties in Judea were the **Pharisees**, known for their strict observance of the Law of Moses and the oral traditions that had developed around it. They believed in the resurrection of the dead and the existence of angels and spirits (Acts 23:8). While smaller in number than the general population, Pharisees commanded significant respect among ordinary Jewish people because of their dedication to Torah study and pious living. They were often the religious teachers (rabbis) in local synagogues, and their interpretations of the Law influenced everyday moral and legal practices.

2. **Sadducees** Another powerful group was the **Sadducees**, comprising mainly the priestly aristocracy and wealthy elites. They controlled the Temple in Jerusalem and administered many aspects of its sacrificial system. In contrast to the Pharisees, Sadducees denied doctrines not explicitly found in the written Torah—such as the resurrection and certain teachings on angels (Mark 12:18; Acts 23:8). Their authority rested on their role in the priesthood and Temple rituals, yet they also sought accommodation with Roman rule to preserve their status and privileges.

3. **Essenes** A somewhat separate, more ascetic sect, the **Essenes** are often associated with the Dead Sea Scrolls and the community at Qumran. While not mentioned by name in the New Testament, historians like Josephus and Philo provide descriptions of their communal lifestyle, which included ritual purity rites, communal meals, and apocalyptic expectations of a future deliverance of Israel (VanderKam & Flint, *The Meaning of the Dead Sea Scrolls*, 2002). The Essenes distanced themselves from what they perceived as a corrupt Temple hierarchy, devoting themselves to preserving sacred texts and preparing for the coming end of the age.

4. **Zealots and Other Revolutionary Groups** Finally, a broader **revolutionary** current ran through segments of Judean society. Groups often labeled **Zealots** or **Sicarii** advocated violent resistance against Roman occupation, dreaming of liberating Judea from pagan control. Some devout Jews saw direct confrontation as the only faithful response to Rome's oppression and its perceived desecration of God's holy land. While not as organized as a single party in Jesus' time, these rebellious factions erupted periodically, culminating in the Great Jewish Revolt (AD 66–70).

The Temple and Its Central Role

At the heart of Judea's religious life stood the **Jerusalem Temple**, originally rebuilt after the Babylonian exile and significantly expanded by Herod the Great. To devout Jews, the Temple was a unique place where God's presence dwelled, and daily sacrifices were offered to uphold the covenant between Israel and God (Deuteronomy 12:5–7). Pilgrimages to the Temple for major feasts such as Passover, Pentecost (Shavuot), and Tabernacles (Sukkot) brought Jews from every corner of the Roman Empire to Jerusalem, reinforcing shared religious identity.

Control over the Temple conferred immense authority. The high priest and his circle, largely Sadducean, oversaw sacrifices, collected tithes, and managed the sacred space. A delicate balance had to be maintained with Roman administrators, who allowed Jewish sacrificial and priestly customs to continue but expected order and loyalty in return. When Jesus drove out money changers and merchants from the Temple courts (Mark 11:15–18), it was not only a religious gesture but also a challenge to those who profited from the Temple economy.

Everyday Life and Cultural Interactions

In addition to religious observances, **everyday life** in first-century Judea revolved around familial and communal relationships. Most people lived in small agrarian communities, farming or working in local trades. Towns like **Nazareth** and **Capernaum**—where Jesus spent significant parts of His early life and ministry—were modest settlements, each with its own synagogue that functioned not just as a religious venue but also as a center for communal gatherings.

Despite the tensions between Jewish sensibilities and Roman authority, there was ongoing cultural interchange. Roads constructed by Rome facilitated travel and commerce. Greek was widely spoken throughout the eastern Mediterranean, which allowed for broader communication. This linguistic environment also set the stage for early Christian writings in **Koine Greek**, bridging cultural gaps between Judea and Hellenistic communities.

2.2 Jewish Concepts of God and Messiah

Monotheism and the Shema

Central to the Jewish religious identity of this era was a **fierce monotheism**, summarized by the **Shema**: "Hear, O Israel: the LORD our God, the LORD is one" (Deuteronomy 6:4). This foundational declaration set Jewish worship apart from the polytheistic practices of surrounding nations. God, understood as the Creator of all that exists, was transcendent, holy, and unique. Yet He was also the God who entered into covenant with Abraham, Isaac, and Jacob, promising to make Israel His chosen people (Genesis 17:7–8). The entire religious system in Judea revolved around fulfilling God's commandments and maintaining fidelity to that covenant.

Such an unshakable monotheism meant that any suggestion of a *human being* claiming divinity would normally be met with **strong opposition**. Scriptural passages like Isaiah 42:8 ("I am the LORD; that is my name; my glory I give to no other") underscored God's exclusivity in receiving worship. Idolatry and polytheism were not merely theological errors; they were sins that threatened the very fabric of Israel's relationship with God. Hence, for someone within this context to be regarded as having divine status was an extraordinary claim that cut to the core of Jewish religious identity (Hurtado, *One God, One Lord*, 1988).

The Nature of God in Jewish Thought

During the Second Temple period (roughly 516 BC to AD 70), Jewish thinkers developed additional ways to talk about the one God, including the concepts of **Wisdom** (Proverbs 8; Wisdom of Solomon), **Word (Memra)** in some Aramaic targums, and **Spirit** as God's active presence. These notions, however, did not displace the cardinal affirmation of monotheism; instead, they provided conceptual frameworks to describe how an utterly transcendent God could engage with creation (Philo of Alexandria offers one such framework in his writings, though he remained a devout monotheist).

Such reflections paved the way for various **messianic speculations**, though not all Jews shared the same perspective on what the Messiah would be like. Some believed the Messiah would be a fully human, anointed king in the line of David, who would re-establish Israel's political freedom and restore the monarchy. Others, possibly influenced by apocalyptic traditions, anticipated a more cosmic or supernatural figure, sometimes described as the "Son of Man," referencing Daniel 7:13–14 (Collins, *The Scepter and the Star*, 1995). Yet even this "Son of Man" language was generally understood within the framework of a God-ordained deliverer, not a second divine being co-equal with God the Father.

Messianic Hopes and Prophetic Expectations

In first-century Judea, **messianic hopes** ran especially high under the weight of Roman occupation. Many devout Jews looked for a deliverer who would overthrow foreign rule and restore the kingdom to Israel (Acts 1:6). The Old Testament prophets had promised a time of renewal and restoration: "For out of Zion shall go the law, and the word of the LORD from Jerusalem" (Isaiah 2:3). In that hope-filled perspective, the Messiah might be a militant king who would defeat Rome, or he might be a divinely empowered priest-king who would purify worship in the Temple and lead a spiritual revival.

This broad spectrum of expectations meant that figures like John the Baptist, who preached repentance and anticipated one mightier than himself (Matthew 3:11), could spark intense interest. Likewise, any teacher performing miracles or gathering disciples could be seen through the lens of fervent messianic speculation. But again, **being the Messiah** was still different from being identified as **God** in the full sense. The idea of the Messiah sharing the unique divine identity, receiving worship, and being an object of devotion was uncommon enough in mainstream Judaism that it typically triggered intense debates—or accusations of blasphemy, should such claims arise explicitly.

Tensions with Traditional Beliefs

When evaluating the question "Is Jesus God?" within Jewish settings of the first century, one must recognize how **countercultural** the notion would have been. Traditional beliefs about God's oneness and the Messiah's role left little room for a *second divine person* walking among humans. Indeed, for most Jews, any addition to the Shema was unthinkable, and worshiping a human figure as divine violated the earliest commandments against idolatry (Exodus 20:3–4). To call Jesus "God" or to attribute to Him the worship due to God alone was, in the eyes of many contemporaries, tantamount to shattering the monotheistic core of Judaism.

Only by appreciating this **theological environment** can one see how truly disruptive it was for the earliest followers of Jesus, themselves devout Jews, to proclaim beliefs that suggested Jesus shared in the identity and prerogatives of Israel's God (Hurtado, *Lord Jesus Christ*, 2003). Later Christian confessions that emerged—claiming that Jesus was not only Messiah but also fully divine—did not arise in a vacuum; they were forged in a milieu where monotheism stood as a defining marker of Jewish faith.

2.3 Greco-Roman Religious Context

A Polytheistic World

Beyond the confines of Judea, the broader Mediterranean world was a **rich tapestry of polytheism**, with ancient gods, local deities, and syncretistic worship practices coexisting in a vibrant religious marketplace. Greek myths had been woven into the cultural fabric for centuries, while Roman conquests introduced a pantheon that often merged or identified Roman gods with their Greek counterparts (e.g., Zeus with Jupiter, Ares with Mars). Temples to various gods peppered the cities of the empire, and devout worshipers might offer sacrifices or prayers at multiple shrines, seeking favor in commerce, agriculture, warfare, or personal affairs.

For the average citizen in the Greco-Roman world, religion was not about exclusive devotion to a single god but rather about **pragmatic**

veneration of those deities believed to hold sway over different aspects of life. The notion of one God who demanded sole allegiance ran counter to these established cultural norms. Even so, certain philosophical schools in the Hellenistic world (like Stoicism) contemplated a singular divine principle or the existence of one supreme deity. While this monotheistic inclination within philosophy sometimes overlapped with Jewish or Christian ideas, it remained a minority position within broader popular religion (Ferguson, *Backgrounds of Early Christianity*, 2003).

Mystery Cults and Religious Syncretism

An important feature of the era was the **mystery cults**, secretive religious groups offering initiates special rites, knowledge, or experiences of divine power. The cult of **Mithras**, for instance, was popular among Roman soldiers, involving elaborate ceremonies that promised cosmic insight or even salvation. The **Eleusinian Mysteries** in Greece and the cult of **Isis** in Egypt also attracted devotees across social strata. These traditions often blended local gods with Greek deities, illustrating the **religious syncretism** that flourished under the vast empire.

Such diversity meant that religious identity was fluid, and new gods or goddesses could be adopted into local pantheons. Local variants of worship practices sprang up, fusing Greek, Roman, Egyptian, and Near Eastern elements. In many city-states, new cults were introduced to gain favor in matters of health or fertility, sometimes building upon or competing with existing temples. This open-ended religious atmosphere posed a stark contrast to Judea's strict monotheism, setting up a cultural clash between Jewish communities (and later Christians) and their polytheistic neighbors.

Emperor Worship

Complicating matters further was the rise of **imperial cults**, where emperors (such as Augustus and his successors) were venerated as divine or semi-divine figures. Over time, offering incense or sacrifices to the emperor's "genius" became a political gesture of loyalty to Rome. Refusal to participate could be interpreted as dissent or even sedition. For communities that upheld an exclusive devotion to one God—such as Jews and early Christians—emperor worship was an unavoidable flashpoint of tension (Wright, *Paul and the Faithfulness of God*, 2013).

Jews were often granted certain exemptions because of the antiquity and recognized status of their religion, at least as long as they prayed for the emperor's well-being in their own way. Early Christians, however, faced suspicion once their movement was perceived as distinct from Judaism. Their refusal to worship the emperor or the Roman gods led to misunderstandings, accusations of atheism (since they did not worship visible gods), and periodic outbreaks of persecution, depending on the attitude of local governors or the policy of the emperor.

The Hellenistic Influence on Thought and Language

Culturally, **Hellenism** had pervaded the eastern Mediterranean since the conquests of Alexander the Great (356–323 BC). Greek language, arts, and philosophies left a deep imprint on almost every urban center. While Latin held sway in administration, Greek remained the lingua franca of trade, diplomacy, and intellectual discourse across the eastern provinces. Philosophical schools— Platonism, Aristotelianism, Stoicism, Epicureanism—offered frameworks for discussing ethics, metaphysics, and the nature of divinity.

When early Christian writers eventually penned the New Testament in **Koine Greek**, they expressed Jewish theological concepts in a language shaped by Hellenistic culture, bridging (and sometimes clashing) with Greek philosophical notions. Phrases like **Logos** (John 1:1) resonated with Greek philosophical ideas about the "rational principle" of the universe, even though its content in

Christian usage carried a distinct Jewish-theological heritage. This interplay between Hebrew monotheism and Hellenistic thought set the stage for Christianity's expansion far beyond Judea.

Crossroads of Cultures

First-century Judea thus existed at the **crossroads of cultures**:

- Rigid monotheism and messianic hope shaped the Jewish sphere.
- Greco-Roman polytheism, emperor worship, and mystery cults characterized the wider empire.
- Political pressures emanated from Rome, with local governors enforcing imperial peace and collecting taxes.
- Linguistic and cultural exchanges occurred through bustling trade routes, which enabled religious ideas to spread swiftly.

Into this mix, **the message about Jesus** would eventually filter out of Judea and into cities like Antioch, Ephesus, Corinth, and Rome. Claims about Jesus being the Messiah might have interested many Jews, while declarations that He was also divine—a "Lord" on par with or even above Caesar—made waves in the Gentile world (Philippians 2:9–11). The environment was ripe for both **conflict** and **rapid growth** of new religious movements, as people sought spiritual answers in a complex and often tumultuous empire (Stark, *The Rise of Christianity*, 1996).

Concluding Thoughts

This chapter has surveyed **first-century Judea**, with its diverse Jewish sects and its pivotal Temple-based worship, alongside the larger **Greco-Roman world**, where polytheistic religions, emperor worship, and philosophical traditions intermixed freely. Within Judea, monotheism was fervently upheld, and messianic hopes ran high under Roman occupation. These Jewish convictions met a starkly different environment in the broader empire, where religious pluralism and syncretism were the norm.

Appreciating this backdrop is crucial for discerning how **early claims about Jesus** would have resonated among different audiences—both Jewish and Gentile. On one side, identifying Jesus with God challenged the central pillar of Jewish monotheism. On the other, proclaiming Him "Lord" in the Roman context risked conflict with the imperial cult and widespread polytheistic assumptions. Indeed, it was in precisely this crucible of overlapping traditions, political tensions, and spiritual yearnings that the message of Jesus' identity began to spread.

As the subsequent chapters will show, the significance of these claims about Jesus and the ensuing developments in early Christian thought cannot be fully grasped apart from an understanding of the **cultural, religious, and political tapestry** that characterized the world in which Jesus lived—and in which His followers first confessed Him as Messiah and, ultimately, **Lord and God** (John 20:28).

Chapter 3: Old Testament Foundations of Divine Identity

3.1 Key Names and Titles of God

The Centrality of God's Names in Ancient Israel

In ancient Israelite religion, a **name** was far more than a convenient label: it expressed the character, essence, or role of the one who bore it. God's revelation of His names in the Hebrew Scriptures thus offered insights into how Israel understood the divine nature and how this understanding laid a basis for later Christological claims.

One of the most critical theological truths embedded in the Old Testament is the absolute uniqueness of Israel's God. He is the Creator of all things (Genesis 1:1), sovereign over history (Isaiah 46:9–10), and the only being worthy of worship (Exodus 20:3–5). This monotheistic conviction distinguished Israel from the surrounding polytheistic nations. The Hebrew Scriptures consistently reinforce the idea that worship of any entity other than

God constitutes idolatry (Deuteronomy 6:13–15).

Given this context, it would have been a revolutionary step for devout Jews to accord the same honor and titles to a **human figure**—unless they were convinced that figure fully shared in God's divine identity. Hence, understanding how God is named and described in the Old Testament is crucial to appreciating why later claims about Jesus' identity evoked both devotion and controversy.

The Tetragrammaton (YHWH)

The most revered name in the Hebrew Bible is the **Tetragrammaton**, spelled **YHWH** (often transliterated "Yahweh"). In Jewish tradition, this name was deemed so sacred that it was rarely pronounced aloud. Instead, readers substituted a term like **Adonai** ("Lord") when encountering YHWH in the biblical text. The meaning of YHWH is often linked to God's self-revelation in Exodus 3:14, "I AM WHO I AM," or "I WILL BE WHO I WILL BE." This declaration conveys God's eternal, self-existent nature— He is the source of all being and exists independently of any external cause (Childs, *The Book of Exodus*, 1974).

When Moses asked God for a name to relay to the Israelites, the response "I AM" emphasized more than mere existence; it implied **ongoing presence**, **sovereignty**, and **faithfulness** to the covenant. By giving Himself this name, God set Israel's concept of the divine apart from the capricious deities of other nations. He was not merely the local god of one city or region but the transcendent and eternal One who governs the entire cosmos.

Elohim and Adonai

Alongside YHWH, the Old Testament uses several other designations for God, such as **Elohim** and **El**. **Elohim** is a plural form in Hebrew but often accompanied by singular verbs when referring to the one God of Israel, indicating a "plural of majesty"

27

rather than suggesting multiple gods. This usage sets the God of Israel apart from other divine assemblies in the ancient Near East, where polytheistic pantheons involved numerous gods of varying ranks (Walton, *Ancient Near Eastern Thought and the Old Testament*, 2006).

Adonai, which literally means "my Lord(s)," is another common title, signifying God's supreme authority over His creation. The significance of Adonai lies partly in its acknowledgment of God's lordship. Ancient Israelites prayed to Adonai as the ultimate sovereign, the One who directs the course of nature and history. While these appellations might initially seem like simple synonyms, they contributed to the tapestry of Israel's understanding of God, emphasizing His power, kingship, covenant faithfulness, and unshared glory.

Implications for Divine Worship

In the religious life of Israel, the name of God demanded reverence. The commandment "You shall not take the name of the LORD your God in vain" (Exodus 20:7) guarded against any misuse or trivialization of God's identity. Worship involved **sacrifice**, **festal celebrations**, and **devotional practices** centered on recognizing God as the holy, transcendent Creator. This profound monotheistic devotion shaped everything from daily prayers to national identity (Deuteronomy 6:4–9).

Therefore, it is crucial to understand how this unwavering commitment to the oneness and uniqueness of YHWH underpins the entire Old Testament. Later, when early Christians began directing worship to Jesus, attributing titles like "Lord" (Greek *Kyrios*) to Him (a title often used for YHWH in the Septuagint), these actions implied that Jesus participates fully in the divine identity otherwise reserved for Israel's God. While the New Testament details those developments, the Old Testament emphasis on the name of God laid a foundation that made the idea of a "divine Messiah" either an

28

unthinkable blasphemy or a startling revelation—depending on one's perspective.

3.2 Messianic Prophecies

Definition and Scope of the Messiah in the Old Testament

The Hebrew word **Mashiach** ("anointed one," from which "Messiah" is derived) primarily refers in the Old Testament to individuals anointed with oil, such as kings (1 Samuel 16:13) or priests (Leviticus 8:12). Over time, Jewish expectations coalesced around a future ideal King—a descendant of David—who would restore Israel's fortunes and usher in an age of peace and righteousness (2 Samuel 7:12–16). These **messianic hopes** began to take on an eschatological dimension, anticipating the fulfillment of God's covenant promises on a cosmic scale (Wright, *The Mission of God*, 2006).

When reading the Old Testament passages traditionally regarded as **messianic prophecies**, one must note that not all texts explicitly mention a "Messiah." Some do, but others present images of an ideal ruler, a suffering servant, or a heavenly figure that later Jewish and Christian interpreters saw as pointing forward to a future redeemer. The Christian perspective retroactively reads these prophecies through the lens of Jesus' life, death, and resurrection, while Jewish interpreters often maintain different understandings. Regardless, the Old Testament provides multiple strands of prophecy suggesting that God's future plans for salvation and global renewal will unfold through a chosen figure intimately related to the Davidic line and the plan of God.

Prophecies of a Royal Deliverer

Among the best-known royal messianic texts is **Isaiah 9:6–7**, which speaks of a child to be born who will have dominion and be called "Wonderful Counselor, Mighty God, Everlasting Father, Prince of

Peace." The titles there—especially "Mighty God" (Hebrew *El Gibbor*)—have spurred significant debate over whether Isaiah intended a direct statement of divinity or a poetic expression of the king's God-empowered rule. From a strictly historical-literal perspective, Isaiah may have been celebrating a Davidic king in his own day or foreseeing an ideal one yet to come.

Yet within the broader canon, the persistent use of exalted language for this figure, who will reign with **justice and righteousness** "from this time forth and forevermore" (Isaiah 9:7), suggests a scope surpassing normal human governance. That is partly why later Jewish tradition, as well as Christian interpreters, identified these verses with a future Messiah (Kaiser, *The Messiah in the Old Testament*, 1995). The promise of an endless reign resonates with God's pledge to David that his dynasty would continue perpetually (2 Samuel 7:13–16).

Similarly, **Jeremiah 23:5–6** refers to a righteous branch from David's line who will "execute justice and righteousness in the land," and whose name will be "The LORD is our righteousness." The Hebrew here—**YHWH Tsidqenu**—once again links the Davidic king with a name that explicitly incorporates the divine Tetragrammaton, highlighting the extraordinary importance of this coming figure. Traditional Jewish exegesis does not necessarily equate that with literal divinity; it could be an honorific or an indication that God's own righteousness will be manifested through the king. However, from a Christian vantage point, these words carry deeper Christological import, suggesting that the Messiah's identity is bound up with the nature and name of YHWH.

The Suffering Servant in Isaiah

Another critical element of messianic expectation appears in the figure of the **Suffering Servant** depicted in **Isaiah 52:13–53:12**. This passage describes a servant who will be "high and lifted up" (Isaiah 52:13), yet also "despised and rejected by men" (53:3). He suffers vicariously, bearing "the iniquity of us all" (53:6) so that many can be accounted righteous (53:11).

In ancient Jewish interpretation, the Servant was sometimes identified with Israel collectively, or with a righteous remnant, or in certain cases with a future messianic individual (e.g., Targum Jonathan applies parts of Isaiah 52:13–53:12 to the Messiah, albeit with interpretive modifications). Later Christian writers, of course, read this "Servant Song" in light of Jesus' crucifixion and resurrection, seeing His atoning death as the ultimate fulfillment of Isaiah's vision.

Although the text does not explicitly label the Servant as divine, the notion of **atoning sacrifice**—something that, in Israel's worship, was typically bound up with the sacrificial system in the Temple— raises the question of how one individual's suffering can effect redemption for others. For Christians, the logic that only God can fully deal with sin converges with the portrayal of a **messianic figure** bearing sins, thus opening the door for a later, more explicit identification of this Suffering Servant with a divine Messiah.

"Son of Man" and Apocalyptic Imagery in Daniel

A further noteworthy passage is the vision of the **"Son of Man"** in **Daniel 7:13–14**. In this apocalyptic scene, the prophet witnesses "one like a son of man" approaching the Ancient of Days (God) and receiving "dominion and glory and a kingdom" so that "all peoples, nations, and languages should serve him." The Aramaic term translated "serve" (*pelach* in Daniel 7:14) can also carry connotations of **worship** or the homage due to a deity (Goldingay, *Daniel*, 1989).

Whether Daniel intended this figure to be seen as divine is debated. Some scholars interpret the "one like a son of man" as a symbol of **faithful Israel** or the saints vindicated after persecution. Yet an alternate stream of Jewish thought, reflected in works like the

Similitudes of Enoch (1 Enoch 37–71), saw the Son of Man as a **preexistent, heavenly figure** enthroned alongside God. In Christian usage, Jesus famously refers to Himself repeatedly as the "Son of Man," and the New Testament links this Danielic imagery to Jesus' authority and divine prerogatives (cf. Mark 14:62).

Consequently, the apocalyptic traditions of late Old Testament and Second Temple Judaism feed into the notion that God might share **rulership** or **authority** with a highly exalted figure, setting the stage for the idea that Jesus, as the Son of Man, could embody more than a purely human role.

Tying the Prophecies Together

When taken as a whole, these Old Testament threads create a **multifaceted portrait** of a future, God-ordained individual or figure who might:

- Reign eternally on David's throne, in alignment with God's own name (Isaiah 9:6–7; Jeremiah 23:5–6).
- Endure suffering on behalf of others, thus securing redemption (Isaiah 52:13–53:12).
- Appear "like a son of man" yet receive universal worship (Daniel 7:13–14).

Taken individually, each passage allows varied interpretations. Yet for later Christians, these prophecies and motifs interlock to reveal a **pattern** that finds fulfillment in Jesus of Nazareth. Still, this interpretation was anything but universally accepted among first-century Jews or beyond, and it required a theological leap: linking a clearly human descendant of David with the divine name and prerogatives of Israel's God, YHWH. How precisely that leap was made in the early Christian community is a matter for later chapters, but it rests on the OT foundations set by passages that hint at a Messiah who transcends the normal boundaries of humanity.

3.3 Bridging the Gap

The Old Testament's Unity of God

One of the essential features of Israel's Scriptures is the strong **affirmation of monotheism**. As discussed in previous sections, the Shema (Deuteronomy 6:4) declares that Israel's God is "one." Furthermore, texts like Isaiah 45:5–6 underscore that there is no other God besides YHWH. This unity was a hallmark of Israel's faith, setting the nation apart from polytheistic neighbors.

Nevertheless, within that unity, the Old Testament occasionally portrays God in ways that allow for a **plurality of expression**—for instance, the **Word** or the **Wisdom** of God as active participants in creation (Proverbs 8:22–31; Psalm 33:6), or the **Angel of the LORD** who sometimes speaks as if He is God Himself (Exodus 3:2–6). While these passages do not fully articulate a doctrine of multiple persons within God, they do raise intriguing possibilities for how God's presence and action could be experienced in distinct modes or agents without violating monotheism (Heiser, *The Unseen Realm*, 2015).

Patterns of God's Self-Revelation

Old Testament narratives contain numerous examples of God **revealing** Himself in specific times and places—through a burning bush (Exodus 3), a pillar of cloud and fire (Exodus 13:21–22), or a still small voice (1 Kings 19:12). These revelations reinforce that the transcendent Creator can become immanent without losing His divine status. In other words, God's **essence** remains unaltered, yet He can genuinely draw near to humanity, whether through physical manifestations or through an anointed individual like a prophet or a king.

When later Christian doctrine suggests that God became incarnate in Jesus Christ, it draws upon an established biblical theme: God is able to **act, speak, and even dwell among His people** in profoundly tangible ways. What's new in Christian teaching is the claim that this time, God not only revealed His presence but took on **full human nature** in the person of Jesus (John 1:14). The Old Testament examples of divine presence and action provide a partial analogy or precursor to such an event, although the concept of incarnation as understood in Christianity remains a significant expansion of these earlier categories.

Moving Toward the Fulfillment: From Expectation to Realization

Israel's story in the Old Testament is one of **promise** and **expectation**. While certain covenants (with Abraham, Moses, David) saw partial fulfillments, the scriptural narrative leaves many threads unresolved:

- Israel repeatedly breaks its covenant, and the prophets foresee judgment and eventual restoration.
- David's heirs fail to establish an enduring righteous monarchy, leading to exile.
- The Temple and sacrificial system, while central to Israel's worship, cannot fully address the nation's ongoing sin and rebelliousness.

The Old Testament thus ends with **tension**: God's character and faithfulness are beyond doubt, but Israel's capacity to live up to the covenant is in question. And yet, from within that story, the texts point forward to a new work of God—a new covenant, a faithful king, a suffering servant, a final deliverance. This forward-looking dimension became a critical platform for early Christian claims that Jesus, in His **life, death, and resurrection**, was the long-awaited culmination of Israel's hopes (Luke 24:25–27).

Christian Reading of Old Testament Foundations

By the time the earliest Christians began proclaiming Jesus as the risen Lord, they looked back into the Hebrew Scriptures and perceived patterns, prophecies, and **types** that found their fulfillment in Him (Romans 1:2–4). They saw Jesus as:

- **Bearing God's holy name** in a way that demanded worship (Philippians 2:9–11).
- **Fulfilling** the royal and prophetic hopes of Isaiah, Jeremiah, and others.
- **Embodied** in the same "I AM" language that defined YHWH in the Old Testament (John 8:58).

Yet these identifications did not form **ex nihilo**; they built on existing biblical frameworks: the majesty of God's name, the potential for the Messiah to exercise divine prerogatives, and God's ability to dwell among His people. While the New Testament extends beyond the Old Testament's explicit statements, it relies heavily on these **foundational motifs**.

Alternative Jewish Understandings

It is worth reiterating that the notion of a **divine Messiah** was not the only way to interpret the Old Testament. Within Judaism, other readings maintained that the Messiah would be a fully human agent. Even texts like Isaiah 9:6–7 could be understood in hyperbolic or regal terms rather than suggesting literal divinity (Kimhi, *Commentary on the Prophets*, 13th century). Moreover, post-biblical Jewish writings often looked for a Messiah who would restore Israel politically and spiritually, yet without collapsing the distinction between the Messiah and God.

Nevertheless, the Old Testament does contain rich and, at times, **sublime** language about God's chosen deliverer, leading some branches of Jewish apocalyptic thought to speculate about a nearly divine or **preexistent** Messiah (as in certain segments of the Enochic tradition). Consequently, the Old Testament, combined with later

Second Temple literature, could be read in ways that allow for a Messiah who transcends typical human limitations—though it was not universal, nor was it the dominant rabbinic perspective that emerged after the destruction of the Temple in AD 70.

A Prelude to the New Testament

All of this underscores that the Old Testament, while unequivocally upholding a **radical monotheism**, also contains theological threads that later **New Testament** authors and early Christians drew upon. They interpreted these threads as pointing to a Messiah who shares in the very identity of YHWH. That is the crux of Old Testament foundations for divine identity:

1. **God's revealed name (YHWH) and titles** illustrate a uniqueness, sovereignty, and holiness that no creature shares.
2. **Messianic prophecies** hint at someone who will bear God's name, bring an everlasting rule, or stand in a unique relationship to the Almighty.
3. **Concepts like God's Word, Wisdom, Spirit, or the Angel of the LORD** reveal a complexity in how God can interact with the created world.
4. **Apocalyptic visions** expand the idea of a heavenly figure who exercises God's own rule and receives universal service.
5. **A story of unresolved tension**—covenantal failure, exile, and the longing for God's ultimate intervention—sets the stage for a climactic moment in salvation history.

While these Old Testament patterns do **not** amount to an explicit and unified doctrine of the Incarnation or the Trinity, they **do** provide categories and anticipations that later made it plausible, for some within Judaism, to accept that the Messiah could indeed be "God with us" (Isaiah 7:14). And from that acceptance emerged the boldest claim of all: that **Jesus, a first-century Jew from Nazareth,** was not only **God's Messiah but truly the incarnate Son of God**—a claim that stands at the heart of Christian worship and theology.

Concluding Thoughts

The Old Testament's portrayal of God leaves no room for worshiping any being other than YHWH. Yet, woven throughout its pages, we find **narratives, prophecies, and poetic imagery** that speak of a divine name, the Suffering Servant, a royal deliverer, and even a heavenly Son of Man. These diverse themes, though open to varied interpretations, collectively form the fertile ground in which the concept of **a divine Messiah** could later take root.

For the earliest Christians, who were themselves faithful Jews, these foundational motifs offered a way to make sense of what they believed God had done in Jesus. They did not see themselves as inventing a new God or breaking faith with Israel's Scriptures; rather, they viewed Jesus as the **full manifestation** of all that the Old Testament had promised yet left unfulfilled.

Chapter 4: Portraits of Jesus in the Gospels

The four Gospels form the **literary heart** of the New Testament. Each offers its own angle on Jesus' life, teaching, miracles, and significance. While they share many core narratives—such as Jesus' baptism, the feeding of the five thousand, certain parables, the Passion story—they also contain unique material and emphasize different themes. Because early Christian tradition recognized these accounts as both authoritative and Spirit-inspired, they became foundational documents for understanding Jesus' identity. In them, we see not just a moral teacher or a Jewish prophet, but someone whose words, deeds, and very presence point to a **unique relationship with God**—one that the rest of the New Testament and the early Church would interpret as **divine**.

This chapter examines the four Gospels one by one, focusing on how each evangelist *portrays* Jesus in ways that support or illuminate the question, "Is Jesus God?" By paying attention to each Gospel's structure, themes, and theological motifs, we gain a richer, more multidimensional appreciation for how the earliest Christians perceived Jesus as sharing in God's very identity.

4.1 Matthew: The Fulfillment of Prophecy

Emphasis on Continuity with the Old Testament

The Gospel of **Matthew** emphasizes Jesus as the **fulfillment of Jewish prophecy** and the climax of Israel's story. From the opening genealogy (Matthew 1:1–17), Matthew situates Jesus firmly in the lineage of Abraham and David, indicating that He embodies the covenant promises made to both. This genealogical introduction highlights Jesus' **royal** and **messianic** credentials: He is "the son of David" (Matthew 1:1), suggesting He is the legitimate heir to David's throne.

Throughout the narrative, Matthew repeatedly draws attention to how Jesus fulfills **Old Testament** prophecies. A common formula appears: "This took place to fulfill what the Lord had spoken by the prophet..." (e.g., Matthew 1:22–23, 2:15, 2:17–18). This rhetorical approach underscores that Jesus does not come out of nowhere but stands as the culmination of centuries of divine revelation. In the eyes of Matthew's community, Jesus is not merely the last in a long line of prophets; He is the **long-awaited Messiah** whose life events align with God's plan recorded in the Hebrew Scriptures.

Jesus as the New Moses and the Divine Teacher

A key motif in Matthew's Gospel is Jesus as the **new Moses** or the ultimate **teacher** of God's people. Matthew structures his Gospel around **five discourses** (Matthew 5–7, 10, 13, 18, 24–25), echoing the five books of the Torah. In the Sermon on the Mount (Matthew 5–7), Jesus interprets the Law from **His own authority**: "You have heard that it was said... but I say to you" (Matthew 5:21–22, 27–28, etc.). This pattern reveals that Jesus is not merely another rabbi commenting on the Law; He speaks as if He has **ultimate interpretive power**, a role that would traditionally belong to God alone.

By **transforming** or clarifying Mosaic commandments in this way, Jesus effectively embodies the divine voice. While earlier prophets said, "Thus says the LORD," Jesus says, "I say to you," implying a direct claim to speak for God without needing an external authority. For Matthew's readers, this would suggest that in Jesus, the **presence** of God and the **fulfillment** of the Torah are uniquely realized.

Immanuel: "God with Us"

Matthew's birth narrative highlights the title **Immanuel**, meaning "God with us" (Matthew 1:22–23, citing Isaiah 7:14). Although ancient Israel believed God was present among His people (e.g., in the Temple), Matthew's application of "God with us" to a **human child** is striking. It implies that in Jesus, **God's own presence** is now tangibly among His people, fulfilling and surpassing earlier signs of divine nearness. The entire Gospel, in fact, is framed by this promise: at the end, the risen Jesus declares, "I am with you always, to the end of the age" (Matthew 28:20). Matthew's Jesus is thus God's personal, abiding presence—a theme that resonates with the question of Jesus' divinity.

4.2 Mark: The Authority of Jesus

The "Messianic Secret" and Progressive Revelation

Mark is often recognized as the earliest written Gospel, characterized by an urgent, fast-paced style. One of Mark's notable features is the so-called **"Messianic Secret."** Time and again, Jesus performs a mighty deed or exorcism and then instructs the beneficiaries or witnesses to **keep silent** about His identity (Mark 1:34, 3:11–12, 8:29–30). Scholars have debated why Mark highlights this pattern. Some propose that Jesus wants to prevent misunderstandings of messiahship; others argue that Mark uses it as a literary device to reveal Jesus' identity **progressively**.

Despite the repeated commands to silence, Mark's narrative reveals that Jesus wields **unprecedented authority**. From the outset (Mark 1:21–28), He teaches in the synagogue and exorcises a demon with a mere command, leading the onlookers to marvel, "What is this? A new teaching—and with authority!" (Mark 1:27). The demon recognizes Jesus as "the Holy One of God," signifying a supernatural awareness of His special status. By highlighting the **exorcisms**, Mark consistently presents Jesus as someone who has power over demonic forces—this level of authority was associated with God's power in Jewish tradition, suggesting that Jesus possesses **God's own dominion** over evil.

Miracles and Claim Over the Sabbath

Mark devotes significant attention to **miracles**—such as healing the sick, feeding the multitudes, and calming storms—which display Jesus' sovereign power over creation. One key episode that underscores Jesus' divine prerogative is found in Mark 2:23–28, where Jesus defends His disciples for plucking grain on the Sabbath. He concludes by declaring, "The Son of Man is lord even of the Sabbath." Given that the Sabbath was instituted by God (Genesis 2:3; Exodus 20:8–11) and seen as a **sign of the covenant**, Mark frames Jesus' claim as an assertion of authority that transcends even the religious laws of Israel. In Mark's portrayal, Jesus is not merely an interpreter of the Law but the ultimate arbiter of divine commandments—a clue that His identity straddles the boundary between the **human** and the **divine**.

The Climactic Confession and the Cross

Mark's Gospel eventually moves toward the climax of Jesus' identity revelation at **Caesarea Philippi** (Mark 8:27–30). Here, Peter confesses Jesus as "the Christ," but Jesus then speaks of **suffering, rejection, and death**—a sequence that confounds the disciples' expectations of a triumphant Messiah. The supreme revelation occurs at Jesus' trial before the high priest, where He admits to being the Christ and prophesies that they will see the "Son of Man seated at the right hand of Power" (Mark 14:62). This reference merges Danielic imagery (Daniel 7:13–14) and Psalm 110:1, hinting that Jesus claims a divine role of cosmic judgment. In Mark's perspective, Jesus' **true identity** can be fully understood only at the cross, where the Roman centurion exclaims, "Truly this man was the Son of God!" (Mark 15:39). This dramatic confession—from a pagan soldier—serves as Mark's final narrative witness to Jesus' divine status.

4.3 Luke: The Savior for All

Universal Scope and Salvation History

While Matthew focuses on Jesus' fulfillment of Jewish expectations and Mark stresses His enigmatic authority, the Gospel of **Luke** presents Jesus as the **Savior for all humanity**. From the start, Luke's narrative highlights marginalized groups—women, the poor, Gentiles—and shows Jesus attending to them with **compassion** (Luke 4:18–19). Luke situates Jesus within a sweeping **salvation history** that moves from Israel's promises to a global mission. For instance, in Luke 2:32, Jesus is depicted as "a light for revelation to the Gentiles, and for glory to your people Israel," bridging Jewish tradition and universal outreach.

Luke's birth narrative amplifies the **divine involvement** in Jesus' origins. The angel Gabriel announces to Mary that the "power of the Most High" will overshadow her, so that the child will be called "the Son of God" (Luke 1:35). Although this phrase can be read in various ways—such as a royal title for Israel's king—Luke implies that Jesus' conception bypasses ordinary means, stressing an unprecedented union of **human** and **divine**. This supernatural inception aligns with the broader question of Jesus' deity: He is uniquely related to God from the moment of His conception.

Prophet, Messiah, and Lord

Luke repeatedly portrays Jesus as a **prophet** in the tradition of Elijah and Elisha (Luke 4:24–27). Yet while Jesus certainly performs prophetic acts like healing and resurrecting the dead, Luke also goes further, depicting Him as the **Messiah** who proclaims "the year of the Lord's favor" (Luke 4:19). One telling moment is the healing of a paralytic in Luke 5:17–26, where Jesus, rather than just pronouncing healing, declares, "Your sins are forgiven." The onlookers ask, "Who can forgive sins but God alone?"—thus raising the possibility that Luke sees Jesus taking on a divine function.

Furthermore, Luke's use of the title **"Lord"** (Greek *kyrios*) for Jesus occurs throughout the narrative. Though *kyrios* can mean "sir" or "master," Luke often gives it a **theological weight** akin to the Old Testament usage for Yahweh in the Greek Septuagint. As early as Luke 2:11, the angelic announcement calls the newborn Jesus "a Savior, who is Christ the Lord." Later, after Jesus' resurrection, Luke shows how the disciples come to recognize Jesus in His glorified state (Luke 24). These references accumulate to portray Jesus not just as a remarkable prophet, but as **the Lord** whose authority and presence continue beyond His earthly life.

The Ascension and the Ongoing Presence of Jesus

Another distinctive element in Luke is the **Ascension** (Luke 24:50–53; Acts 1:6–11, also authored by Luke). This event depicts Jesus being taken up into heaven, signifying His exaltation and continued **lordship** over the world. By locating the Ascension at the end of the Gospel (and expanding on it in Acts), Luke emphasizes that Jesus' ministry on earth transitions into a **heavenly reign**, from which He directs the growth and mission of the early Church. This theological move accentuates Jesus' participation in **God's own sovereignty**, an idea that resonates strongly with the question of His divinity.

4.4 John: The Word Made Flesh

High Christology from the Outset

The Gospel of **John** stands out for its **explicit** depiction of Jesus' **divine identity**. Unlike the Synoptics (Matthew, Mark, Luke), which begin with a birth narrative or early ministry, John opens with a **prologue** (John 1:1–18) that speaks of the eternal **Word (Logos)** who "was with God" and "was God." This Word "became flesh and dwelt among us" (John 1:14). The theological weight of this opening is immense: it identifies Jesus as the **preexistent** divine agent of creation (John 1:3).

By placing Jesus "in the beginning" and equating Him with God's creative word, John signals that this is no mere teacher or prophet. The radical claim is that Jesus shares in **God's very being** yet has entered history as a real human being. This concept of the Incarnation—God taking on human flesh—lies at the heart of John's portrait. Even before John recounts any of Jesus' actions, he anchors Him in God's eternal existence, shaping how every subsequent episode should be interpreted.

The "I Am" Sayings and Signs

John's Gospel is also famous for its series of **"I am"** sayings, such as "I am the bread of life" (John 6:35), "I am the light of the world" (8:12), and "I am the resurrection and the life" (11:25). While each statement highlights an aspect of Jesus' ministry—sustenance, illumination, life-giving power—they collectively evoke the divine self-revelation of the Old Testament (Exodus 3:14), where God declares Himself as "I AM WHO I AM." John intensifies this association in passages like John 8:58, where Jesus says, "Before Abraham was, I am," prompting an attempt by His listeners to stone Him for **blasphemy**.

Likewise, John structures his narrative around **signs**—miracles that reveal Jesus' glory and elicit faith. From turning water into wine at Cana (John 2:1–11) to raising Lazarus from the dead (John 11:1–

44), each sign underscores a divine dimension to Jesus. These are not just wonders to help people in need; they are **manifestations** of Jesus' identity as the **Son of God**. The climactic sign is Jesus' own resurrection, after which Thomas confesses, "My Lord and my God!" (John 20:28). That John's Gospel ends with this exclamation encapsulates how the evangelist wants his readers to see Jesus: not just as Messiah, but as **God** in the fullest sense.

Relationship with the Father and the Spirit

John further develops the theme of Jesus' intimate **relationship with the Father**, insisting that "the Son can do nothing of his own accord, but only what he sees the Father doing" (John 5:19). Jesus speaks of a unity of **will**, **purpose**, and **essence** with the Father, culminating in statements like, "I and the Father are one" (John 10:30). While this unity is sometimes interpreted as a unity of intention, the reaction of the religious leaders—who again accuse Jesus of blasphemy (John 10:31–33)—indicates they understand it as a claim to **equality with God**.

John's Gospel also highlights the **Holy Spirit**, who is promised by Jesus as the "Helper" or "Advocate" (John 14:16–17). Though John does not give a complete Trinitarian formula, he strongly suggests a **triadic** relationship: the Father, the Son, and the Spirit acting in concert, especially in the context of salvation and revelation (John 14–16). Thus, John's portrait of Jesus is the most overtly **"high Christology"** among the Gospels, leaving little doubt that the community behind John's writings considered Jesus fully divine while also fully human.

Concluding Thoughts

While **Matthew**, **Mark**, **Luke**, and **John** each offer distinct angles on Jesus' life and significance, their portraits converge on the central theme that He is **no ordinary human being**. Matthew underscores

Jesus as **Immanuel**, the fulfillment of Old Testament prophecies and the new Moses who speaks with God's authority. Mark paints Him as a mysteriously powerful figure whose *messianic secret* gradually unfolds until the cross and the confession that He is the **Son of God**. Luke presents Him as the **Savior for all humanity**, bridging the gap between Jews and Gentiles, and highlighting His role as both prophet and exalted Lord. Lastly, John delivers the most explicit declaration of Jesus' **divine identity**, proclaiming Him the eternal Word made flesh and culminating in Thomas's address to the risen Jesus as "My Lord and my God!"

In all four Gospels, the narratives push beyond a mere claim that Jesus was a **teacher, healer, or social reformer**. Instead, they demonstrate that the earliest Christian communities regarded Him as sharing in God's own nature—fulfilling ancient hopes, exercising divine authority, and ultimately deserving the worship due only to the **one God** of Israel. Each apostles deploys a unique literary and theological approach, but together they create a **multifaceted tapestry** that invites readers to respond to Jesus as both **Messiah** and **Lord**. Far from contradicting one another, these four portraits reinforce the overarching claim that Jesus, while truly human, **embodies the very presence of God** among His people.

Chapter 5: Examining Jesus' Own Claims

5.1 Implicit Declarations

Using Divine Titles or Names Associated with Yahweh

One of the central questions about Jesus' divinity involves whether He ever explicitly referred to Himself as **God** or whether He used terminology closely tied to God's identity in the Hebrew Scriptures. While Jesus does not say the English phrase "I am God" in the Gospel narratives, scholars argue that He employed language and titles that often carried **divine connotations** within a Jewish milieu (Wright, *Jesus and the Victory of God*, 1996). In the first century, **God** was primarily referring to God the Father.

A prominent example is Jesus' repeated use of the phrase **"I am"** (Greek *egō eimi*) in the Gospel of John. In John 8:58, Jesus declares, "Before Abraham was, I am." Many interpret this statement in light of Exodus 3:14, where God reveals His name as "I AM WHO I AM." Those who heard Jesus—particularly Jewish religious leaders—understood this phrase as potentially blasphemous because it evoked the **sacred Tetragrammaton (YHWH)**. They even attempted to stone Him (John 8:59), indicating they perceived His statement as a claim to divine identity. Although some critics argue that "I am" might simply denote existence prior to Abraham, the violent reaction suggests that Jesus' listeners heard in His words an allusion to God's *self-revelatory* name (Carson, *The Gospel According to John*, 1991).

Another example involves the title **"Son of Man."** At first glance, the phrase may sound like a declaration of humanity. However, in a first-century Jewish context, "Son of Man" could carry profound eschatological and possibly divine overtones, drawn in part from Daniel 7:13–14. In that prophetic vision, "one like a son of man" is granted authority and an everlasting dominion that transcends normal human reigns. Jesus repeatedly used this title in contexts where He spoke about judging the world (e.g., Matthew 25:31–46) or returning in glory, effectively linking Himself to the heavenly figure who receives worship and universal rule in Daniel's prophecy.

Jesus' Relationship with the Father

Another way Jesus made implicit declarations of divinity was by describing a **unique relationship** with God the Father—one that set Him apart from prophets or righteous individuals who simply do God's will. Repeatedly, Jesus calls God **"my Father"** rather than using more communal language such as "our Father" (in certain contexts). For instance, in John 5:17–18, after healing a man on the Sabbath, Jesus says, "My Father is working until now, and I am working." The text clarifies that the Jewish leaders sought to kill Him because "He was even calling God his own Father, making himself equal with God." Within a monotheistic Jewish framework, claiming such an intimate equivalence with the Father pointed to a divine self-understanding rather than simply a prophet's reverence for God.

Moreover, in John 10:30, Jesus proclaims, "I and the Father are one." This statement triggered another attempt by His opponents to stone Him for **blasphemy** (John 10:31–33). They plainly charge: "You, a mere man, make yourself God." While various interpreters debate the nuances of "one" (Greek *hen*), the violent response from the crowd indicates they interpreted His words as a claim of unity in essence with the God of Israel. They did not see Jesus merely as claiming a close alignment of purpose but as staking a claim that intruded into **God's unique domain**.

Taken together, these implicit declarations—references to "I AM," the usage of "Son of Man" in an exalted sense, and the assertion of oneness with the Father—strongly contributed to the early Christian understanding that Jesus shared in the divine identity. Even if Jesus refrained from a straightforward statement like "I am God" in modern English terms, the cultural and theological contexts show that His audience often reacted as though He had claimed far more than human authority.

5.2 Authority Over the Law and Sabbath

Challenging Pharisaic Interpretations

In the Gospels, Jesus frequently engages in disputes with the **Pharisees**, who were renowned for their meticulous observance of the Mosaic Law and additional oral traditions. One of the most striking aspects of these confrontations is how Jesus speaks about the **Law**—not merely as a teacher or interpreter but as someone who **possesses an inherent authority** to clarify or even supersede certain traditional understandings.

For instance, during the **Sermon on the Mount** (Matthew 5–7), Jesus repeatedly uses the formula: "You have heard that it was said... but I say to you." These antitheses address issues such as anger, adultery, oaths, retaliation, and love for enemies. While Jesus does not contradict the Law outright, He often penetrates beyond the external requirements to expose the heart-level demands of righteousness, a perspective that can transform or heighten the

Law's expectations. Importantly, He does so on **His own authority**, not citing the revered rabbis or disclaiming: "Thus says the Lord," as Old Testament prophets often did. This rhetorical move implies a **self-assumed position of divine spokesperson**—or more than that, a direct expression of God's intent.

Additionally, in Mark 2:23–28, Jesus' disciples pluck grain on the Sabbath, prompting Pharisaic critique. Jesus defends them by recalling how David ate the consecrated bread but then makes a bolder claim: "The Son of Man is Lord even of the Sabbath." Within Judaism, the Sabbath was an institution given by God Himself—a sign of the covenant (Exodus 31:13). Therefore, to declare lordship **over** the Sabbath is tantamount to asserting a place above or equal to the divine Lawgiver. As a result, the religious authorities would have viewed Jesus' statement as radically innovative if not outright scandalous.

Statements That Imply a Divine Prerogative

Throughout the Synoptic Gospels (Matthew, Mark, Luke), Jesus not only reinterprets certain laws but also **pardons sin**—arguably an even more explicit claim to divine prerogative. In Mark 2:1–12, for example, a paralytic is brought to Jesus, and He tells the man, "Son, your sins are forgiven." Scribes present reason within themselves: "Why does this man speak like that? He is blaspheming! Who can forgive sins but God alone?" Indeed, in Jewish tradition, the forgiveness of sins—especially in a final, absolute sense—was God's domain. Prophets might declare that God forgives sin, but for Jesus to speak in the first-person singular implies that the authority to forgive sin resided **with Him**.

The subsequent miracle of healing the paralytic adds dramatic proof to Jesus' claim: "But that you may know that the Son of Man has authority on earth to forgive sins…" (Mark 2:10–11). The man then stands up and walks. The rhetorical effect is clear: Jesus demonstrates supernatural authority through healing, corroborating

His right to **pronounce forgiveness**—a right that had hithertofore been ascribed only to the Lord of Israel.

Furthermore, Jesus frequently **reinterprets or refocuses** commandments in ways that highlight His sense of personal authority. He critiques certain Pharisaic traditions (e.g., Mark 7:1–13) for nullifying the intent of God's command. And while He upholds the ultimate **moral vision** of the Law (Mark 12:28–34), the way He speaks as one who discerns and dictates divine will underscores that His position is more than that of a mere human rabbi. He acts as though He is unveiling God's original design in a manner only the Lawgiver could do.

5.3 The Trial Before the Jewish Leaders

Significance of the High Priest's Question and Jesus' Response

The Jesus' identity comes to a head during His **trial** before the Jewish council (often referred to as the Sanhedrin). In the Gospel of Mark (14:53–65), Jesus is confronted by the High Priest, who presses Him: "Are you the Christ, the Son of the Blessed?" Such a question encapsulates not merely whether Jesus was a political or military messiah but whether He was claiming a **unique filial relationship** with God—an audacious stance in that Jewish setting if it implied equality with God.

Jesus responds, "I am, and you will see the Son of Man seated at the right hand of Power, and coming with the clouds of heaven" (Mark 14:62). This answer fuses elements from Daniel 7:13–14 (the exalted Son of Man) and Psalm 110:1 (the enthroned figure at God's right hand). By placing Himself within these exalted scriptures, Jesus proclaims a role far beyond an earthly king's. The High Priest reacts by tearing his garments and accusing Jesus of **blasphemy**. In the High Priest's eyes, Jesus has effectively elevated Himself to a station belonging solely to God.

Many modern interpreters debate the **scope** of this claim: Did Jesus simply foresee a vindication by God, or did He outright declare equality with the Almighty? In the Jewish legal context, the High Priest's extreme response suggests the latter. Additionally, the language of "coming with the clouds of heaven" was loaded with **divine connotations**, often referencing God's glory and presence (cf. Exodus 13:21, Daniel 7:13). Hence, the trial narratives portray a climactic moment in which the religious authorities conclude that Jesus' self-identification is offensive enough to warrant capital punishment.

Accusations of Blasphemy and Their Implications

Under Jewish law, **blasphemy** typically involved either cursing God directly or, at times, usurping God's prerogatives (Mishnah, *Sanhedrin* 7:5). It was considered a grave offense punishable by death. From the perspective of the Sanhedrin's leadership, Jesus seemed to be doing precisely that—claiming for Himself titles and roles associated with YHWH. Even if the biblical or rabbinic definitions of blasphemy could be interpreted in various ways, it is clear that the **authorities** saw Jesus' claims as deeply subversive and theologically unacceptable.

As a result, they handed Jesus over to the Roman governor, Pontius Pilate, accusing Him of sedition and of claiming to be a king in opposition to Caesar. But the core religious charge was that He had made Himself **equal to God** (John 19:7), an accusation that strongly echoes the earlier conflicts in the Gospel narratives. For the Gospel writers, this condemnation by the Jewish leadership was ironically the ultimate testimony to Jesus' *true identity*: they crucified Him precisely because they recognized that He claimed the prerogatives of God. Whether or not they believed His claim, they at least recognized it **was** His claim.

Concluding Thoughts

Across the Gospels, Jesus' *own words and actions* form the backbone of the Christian claim that He is God incarnate. While He never uses the precise contemporary phrasing "I am God" in the Synoptic or Johannine accounts, He frequently employs language that **alludes to God's unique identity** in the Hebrew Scriptures. He refers to Himself as "I am," evokes the role of the "Son of Man" from Daniel 7, and speaks of His unity with the Father in ways that provoke accusations of **blasphemy** from those around Him.

In addition, Jesus **exercises authority over the Mosaic Law**, redefines or reaffirms commandments on His own say-so, and claims to forgive sins—actions the Jewish religious leaders understood as divine prerogatives. Such bold gestures are most starkly displayed in statements like "The Son of Man is Lord of the Sabbath" and in the climactic trial scene where He confesses to the High Priest that He is indeed the Christ and will be seen at God's right hand. These claims collectively underscore that Jesus saw Himself as more than a prophet or teacher; He implied a divinity that shared in the identity and authority of Israel's God.

The direct responses of His contemporaries—whether in calls for His **execution** or in worship by His followers—reveal how these statements were interpreted within the first-century Jewish context. Jesus' opponents recognized (and rejected) an implicit or explicit claim to divinity, while His disciples embraced it as central to their faith. Subsequent Christian theology would reflect deeply on these moments, eventually articulating doctrines like the Incarnation and the Trinity to explain how Jesus could be both fully human and fully God. The foundations for these doctrines, however, rest in the **Gospel accounts** themselves, where Jesus' own words and deeds point toward a **divine self-understanding** that challenged the world around Him and continues to shape Christian belief to this day.

Chapter 6: Demonstrations of Divine Power

The Gospels depict Jesus performing numerous miracles, acts that go beyond ordinary human capacity and thereby suggest a **supernatural authority** at work. Historically, prophets and miracle workers also appeared in the Jewish tradition—for example, Moses parted the Red Sea (Exodus 14:21–22), and Elijah multiplied flour and oil for a starving widow (1 Kings 17:14–16). Nonetheless, the **scale, manner, and theological significance** of Jesus' miracles set them apart in several ways. First, He does not typically invoke God's name or perform elaborate ritual gestures; rather, He acts by **His own command**. Second, many of His miracles reflect authority over domains associated with God alone (nature, evil spirits, human life and death). Third, the Gospel writers use these events to underscore Jesus' identity, hinting that in Him, God's very presence has arrived among His people.

From turning water into wine at a wedding feast (John 2:1–11) to commanding the stormy sea to be still (Mark 4:39), Jesus' miracles range from acts of **compassion**—healing the sick or freeing the demon-possessed—to displays of **sovereign power** that echo the divine actions celebrated in Israel's Scriptures. These mighty works are typically followed by a sense of awe in onlookers, who exclaim, "Who then is this?" (Mark 4:41). At times, the crowds even ask whether Jesus might be a prophet "like one of the prophets of old" (Mark 6:15), yet the cumulative effect of His miracles suggests He is more than a prophet. This chapter explores three major categories of Jesus' demonstrations of divine power: **authority over nature, authority over illness and demonic oppression, and ultimately the resurrection—often seen by Christians as the crowning evidence of His divine status**.

6.1 Miracles and Authority Over Nature

Calming the Storm and Walking on Water

In the Synoptic Gospels (Matthew, Mark, and Luke), one of the most striking demonstrations of Jesus' mastery over nature is **calming a violent storm** on the Sea of Galilee (Mark 4:35–41; Matthew 8:23–27; Luke 8:22–25). Jesus, asleep in the boat, is awakened by His terrified disciples. He rebukes the wind and commands the sea, "Peace! Be still!" (Mark 4:39). Immediately, the waves cease, and a great calm settles upon the waters. The disciples' reaction is one of profound astonishment: "Who then is this, that even the wind and the sea obey him?" (Mark 4:41). In the Hebrew Bible, controlling the chaotic forces of nature—particularly the sea—was often ascribed to God alone. Passages like Psalm 89:9 extol God: "You rule the raging of the sea; when its waves rise, you still them." By echoing this language, Mark and the other evangelists hint that Jesus is exercising a divine prerogative.

A related miracle that further underscores Jesus' unusual sovereignty is His **walking on water** (Mark 6:45–52; Matthew 14:22–33; John 6:16–21). This event occurs in the early morning hours, with the disciples struggling against strong winds. Jesus appears, walking across the waves toward their boat. In Matthew's account, Peter also attempts to walk on water but falters in fear. Jesus rescues him, and upon entering the boat, the wind ceases. The disciples worship Him, saying, "Truly you are the Son of God" (Matthew 14:33). Once again, the underlying **theology** is unmistakable: treading upon the sea is an image found in Job 9:8, which praises God as the One who "tramples the waves of the sea." The evangelists thus portray Jesus as operating in a realm that Jewish Scripture had traditionally reserved for Yahweh alone.

Feeding the Multitudes

Another nature-based miracle is the **feeding of the five thousand** (Mark 6:30–44; Matthew 14:13–21; Luke 9:10–17; John 6:1–14), which is the only miracle recorded in all four Gospels. With just five loaves and two fish, Jesus provides enough food to satisfy a large crowd, leaving twelve baskets of leftovers. The event echoes God's provision of manna in the wilderness (Exodus 16) and the prophetic multiplication of oil and flour by Elijah and Elisha (1 Kings 17:14–16; 2 Kings 4:42–44). However, the scope here is immense, with thousands fed in one sitting. John's Gospel (6:14–15) emphasizes that the crowd perceives Jesus as the "Prophet who is to come into the world," recalling Deuteronomy 18:15–18—a prophecy about a future figure like Moses. Yet Jesus is not simply distributing supernaturally provided bread; He is, in the broader Johannine context, **the Bread of Life** (John 6:35), revealing a connection between the physical miracle and a deeper spiritual reality.

The Wedding at Cana

While the Synoptics highlight dramatic encounters with nature, John's Gospel opens Jesus' public ministry with the **wedding at Cana** (John 2:1–11), where He turns water into wine. John refers to this as the "first of his signs" (John 2:11), revealing Jesus' **glory**. On the surface, the transformation of water to wine might not appear as grandiose as stilling a storm or multiplying loaves. Yet it underscores Jesus' **creative power**—He brings about a transformation in substance that not only solves a social dilemma (running out of wine) but also demonstrates the abundant, joyous character often associated with divine blessing (Amos 9:13–14). John's language about "signs" serves as an interpretive framework throughout his Gospel, pointing to Jesus' identity as the One through whom the Father is revealed (John 1:18).

Implications for Divine Identity

Collectively, these miracles of dominion over nature bear an unmistakable theological weight: they position Jesus not merely as a prophet or righteous teacher, but as an agent—and even the **source**—of divine power. In ancient Judaism, the sea represented **chaos**, only subdued by God at creation (Genesis 1:2–10) or through miraculous acts (Psalm 77:16–19). Providing bread in the wilderness also echoed the **Exodus tradition**, where God sustained Israel with manna. Thus, the Gospels interpret these miracles as signs that Jesus stands in the **place of God**, fulfilling and surpassing earlier biblical motifs. While critics might argue that later Christian theology read too much into these episodes, the narratives themselves—complete with Old Testament allusions—invite readers to see Jesus' wonders as **evidence of God's presence** in their midst.

6.2 Healing and Exorcisms as a Divine Sign

Jesus' Unique Approach to Healing

While ancient prophets and holy people could pray for or enact miraculous cures (2 Kings 5:1–14), Jesus' **healing ministry** in the Gospels stands out for both its **sheer abundance** and its **directness**. In many episodes, He touches the sick or even heals them from a distance by speaking a word (Matthew 8:5–13). Crowds bring the lame, blind, and paralyzed to Him, and the Gospels repeatedly mention that Jesus "healed them all" (e.g., Matthew 12:15). Rather than elaborate rituals, He frequently uses a short command: "Be clean" (Mark 1:41), "Receive your sight" (Luke 18:42).

These uncomplicated methods reflect **inherent authority**: Jesus does not conjure or plead; He issues directives that reality obediently follows. Moreover, His compassion stands at the center of many accounts (Matthew 9:36, Mark 1:41), linking divine power with **divine mercy**—characteristics ascribed to God throughout the Hebrew Scriptures (Psalm 145:8–9). Some commentators point out that Jesus' healings, especially of lepers and the ritually unclean, symbolize a new era of **holiness** that goes out from Him to cleanse impurity, rather than the other way around (Wenham, *The Concept of Purity in the Bible*, 1970).

Exorcisms and the Defeat of Evil Powers

Exorcisms form another core component of Jesus' miraculous activity. The Gospels frequently portray Him **expelling demons** or unclean spirits with a simple rebuke: "Come out of him!" (Mark 5:8). In Mark 1:27, onlookers exclaim, "What is this? A new teaching—and with authority! He commands even the unclean spirits, and they obey him." In the Jewish worldview of the period, demonic oppression was a grim reality signifying the presence of **hostile spiritual forces**. While other exorcists might invoke God or angels as mediators, Jesus commands demons **directly**, as though He possesses an inherent right to do so.

Particularly dramatic is the account of the **Gerasene demoniac** (Mark 5:1–20), a man tormented by a legion of demons. The demons beg Jesus not to torment them, recognizing His authority to cast them into the abyss. By sending them into a herd of pigs that then rushes into the sea, Jesus liberates the man entirely. The incident underscores that even a legion of hostile spirits is powerless against His command.

From a theological perspective, these **exorcisms** manifest the inbreaking of God's kingdom, a sign that **Satan's dominion** is being overthrown. In Matthew 12:28, Jesus declares, "But if it is by the Spirit of God that I cast out demons, then the kingdom of God has come upon you." By casting out demons in His own name, Jesus shows an **authority inherent within Himself**—an authority that, according to early Christian belief, belongs to God alone (cf. Luke 11:20, which has "finger of God" in place of "Spirit of God," reinforcing the direct link to divine power).

Reactions of the Crowds and Religious Leaders

Healing and exorcisms not only impact the individuals rescued but also provoke **public astonishment** and debate. Crowds often glorify God, acknowledging that "a great prophet" has arisen (Luke 7:16), or they simply marvel at Jesus' power. Meanwhile, certain religious authorities in the Gospels accuse Him of **collaborating with demonic forces** (Mark 3:22). Jesus counters this accusation by illustrating the illogic of Satan casting out his own agents. The friction shows that not everyone found Jesus' miracles convincing or welcomed His implicit claim to divine authority. Instead, His works became a flashpoint, forcing onlookers to choose whether to interpret these displays as evidence of God's presence or as a deceptive power.

Significance for Understanding Jesus' Divinity

In the broader tapestry of the Gospels, healings and exorcisms are woven together with Jesus' teaching, parables, and interactions with various social groups. Yet these miraculous acts serve as **tangible demonstrations** of the claim that **God's reign** is breaking into history through Jesus. It is one thing for Jesus to teach with lofty authority; it is another for Him to **transform** lepers into healthy men and women or to **drive out** malevolent spirits. Ancient Israel's prophets performed miracles in the name of the Lord, but Jesus repeatedly acts **by His own inherent power**, thus bridging the line between a messenger of God and the embodiment of God's authority.

6.3 Resurrection and Divine Vindication

The Centrality of the Resurrection in Christian Faith

While Jesus' miracles over nature and sickness are profound, the **resurrection** stands as the **crowning demonstration** of His divine identity within Christian belief. According to the New Testament, Jesus was **crucified** under Pontius Pilate but rose from the dead on the third day, appearing to many of His followers (1 Corinthians 15:3–8). This event is not merely an example of miraculous power; it is the **theological linchpin** of Christianity. As the Apostle Paul candidly states, "If Christ has not been raised, then our preaching is in vain and your faith is in vain" (1 Corinthians 15:14).

From a historical standpoint, the empty tomb and the reported **post-resurrection appearances** spurred the earliest disciples to proclaim that Jesus was exalted at God's right hand. The Gospels narrate scenes where He appears to individuals (Mary Magdalene, John 20:11–18) and groups (the disciples, Luke 24:36–49), defying the finality of death. The resurrection narratives present Jesus as **physically transformed**—He can pass through locked doors, yet He also eats fish with His followers (Luke 24:41–43). This paradoxical combination of continuity (His wounded hands and feet) and transformation underscores the claim that a **new mode of existence** has broken into human history.

Resurrection as God's Seal of Approval

In the religious context of first-century Judea, a **crucified Messiah** was a contradiction in terms. Most Jews expected the Messiah to triumph over foreign oppression, not die under it. Yet Jesus' resurrection, according to the earliest Christians, reversed the verdict of His executioners, revealing that **God had validated** both Jesus' mission and His claims to divine authority (Romans 1:4). In other words, the resurrection was the divine **"stamp of approval"**—Jesus was not another failed revolutionary but the very **Son of God** who overcame sin and death. Early Christian preaching (e.g., Peter's sermon in Acts 2:22–36) consistently points to the resurrection as the definitive sign that Jesus is Lord.

This notion of **divine vindication** has parallels in certain Jewish texts that describe the suffering of the righteous and their ultimate exaltation by God (Wisdom of Solomon 5:1–5). Nonetheless, the Christian claim that Jesus physically rose and now reigns at God's side introduced a **radical dimension**—He was not only vindicated but was also elevated to a position that early Christian confession equated with sharing in God's **unique sovereignty** (Philippians 2:9–11). Instead of being "just" a miracle, the resurrection is portrayed as the **inauguration** of a new creation, an event where the boundary between mortal life and divine glory is transcended in the person of Jesus.

The Appearance of the Risen Lord

Each of the Gospels concludes with resurrection appearances, and the Book of Acts begins with Jesus **spending forty days** with His disciples before ascending into heaven (Acts 1:3–11). The variety of these appearances—Mary Magdalene at the tomb, the disciples on the road to Emmaus, the group by the Sea of Galilee—suggests that belief in the resurrection was **not** based on a single, isolated incident. Instead, multiple experiences convinced Jesus' followers that He was truly alive. Even skeptics like Thomas (John 20:24–29) were invited to **examine the wounds** as proof. Many scholars note that such accounts are not easily explained by simple categories of hallucination or legend, given the diversity and collective nature of these reported encounters (Wright, *The Resurrection of the Son of God*, 2003).

Within the Gospels, these appearances often culminate in **worship**. For instance, in Matthew 28:9, the risen Jesus meets some of the disciples, and they "took hold of his feet and worshiped him." This reaction resonates with the biblical teaching that **worship is due to God alone** (Deuteronomy 6:13), suggesting that by bowing before Jesus, the disciples recognize in Him the very presence of the divine. This worship aspect, combined with the claim of physical resurrection, forms a powerful basis for subsequent Christian theology: if Jesus overcame death and receives the worship due God, He must indeed share in God's nature.

Implications for Divine Identity

Thus, for early Christians, the resurrection **confirmed** all that Jesus had claimed and accomplished during His ministry. By conquering death—an act that throughout Scripture is associated uniquely with God as the author of life (Psalm 36:9)—Jesus demonstrated that He possessed **life in Himself** (cf. John 5:26). If the feeding of the multitudes and calming the storm signaled authority over nature, and if healings and exorcisms signaled authority over sickness and evil, then the resurrection pointed to an authority even over **the grave**.

Early Christian preaching (Acts 2:24, 3:15) repeatedly emphasizes that death could not hold Jesus, aligning with the Old Testament's notion that God alone has the ultimate say over life and death (Deuteronomy 32:39). That Jesus exercised such authority in His own resurrection, rather than merely serving as a passive recipient, led His followers to worship Him as **the exalted Lord**. While controversies over the historical details of the resurrection persist, the textual witness is clear that for the New Testament authors—and the first generations of Christians—**this** was the decisive proof that Jesus was more than a teacher or prophet. He was, as Thomas confessed, "My Lord and my God!" (John 20:28).

Concluding Thoughts

Throughout His ministry, Jesus performed miracles that **defied**

natural laws, from calming storms and walking on water to multiplying bread for massive crowds. He **healed** incurable diseases and **drove out** demonic powers with a simple command, displaying a mastery over both the physical and spiritual realms. While Old Testament prophets had wrought wonders in God's name, Jesus' miracles were often **executed by His own word**, suggesting a personal authority indistinguishable from the divine. These acts challenged onlookers to interpret **who** could wield such power.

At the culmination of the Gospel story, Jesus' **resurrection** from the dead emerges as the ultimate demonstration of divine power. Early believers saw it not merely as a grand miracle but as the **foundation** of their confession that Jesus is indeed **Lord**. Within the Jewish framework that reserved worship for God alone, the disciples' worship of the risen Jesus signaled that they recognized in Him the very life and authority of God. By **defeating death** and claiming victory over the forces of evil, Jesus fulfilled scriptural hopes that only God Himself could bring about such comprehensive deliverance.

Taken together, these demonstrations—miracles of nature, healings, exorcisms, and the resurrection—form a core pillar of the Christian conviction that Jesus shares in the identity of Israel's God. They are not isolated wonders but **signposts** pointing to who He is. Even critics who question the historical literalness of each miracle acknowledge that the Gospel writers present these episodes as evidence of a **divine mission**. For Christian readers through the centuries, these narratives reinforce the central claim of the faith: in Jesus, God walked among us, and His power overflowed into tangible acts of compassion, restoration, and victory over death itself.

Chapter 7: Witness and Testimony in the Early Church

The question "Is Jesus God?" did not end with Jesus' resurrection or the Gospel accounts. On the contrary, the **earliest Christian communities** continued to wrestle with, proclaim, and define their understanding of Jesus' divine identity in the face of both Jewish and Gentile critiques. The New Testament letters, along with other first- and second-century Christian documents, shed light on how believers articulated their faith. Far from being a marginal aspect of Christian devotion, the recognition of Jesus as **divine** sat at the center of the Church's message and life, shaping doctrinal confessions, liturgical worship, and the entire trajectory of Christian missionary activity.

This chapter looks at three interrelated dimensions of early Christian testimony: the **Apostolic Proclamation**, which rooted its message in the disciples' encounters with the risen Christ; the **Worship of Jesus**, which evolved in a distinctly Christocentric direction; and the **Expansion of Early Christianity**, which saw the faith spread rapidly throughout the Mediterranean world, propelled by the conviction that in Jesus, God's own presence had decisively entered history.

7.1 Apostolic Proclamation

Peter's Sermons and the Core Kerygma

Among the key sources for understanding how the earliest Church perceived Jesus are the **sermons** in the Book of Acts, particularly those attributed to the Apostle Peter. In Acts 2:22–36, Peter addresses a crowd in Jerusalem shortly after Pentecost. He proclaims that Jesus, crucified by human hands, has been vindicated by God through resurrection and exaltation to God's right hand. Peter's conclusion that "God has made him both Lord and Christ" (Acts 2:36) demonstrates a core Christian conviction:

1. Jesus is the awaited **Messiah (Christ)** of Israel.
2. As "Lord," He holds a status of divine authority, echoing the Old Testament reference to Yahweh as Lord.

Although the Greek word *kyrios* ("Lord") can sometimes simply mean "master" or a person of high status, in the Septuagint (the Greek translation of the Hebrew Bible), *kyrios* is the standard rendering of **YHWH**. By applying *kyrios* to Jesus—and doing so in contexts that overlap with worship—Peter and the early preachers were effectively placing Jesus **in the sphere of divine identity**. They also interpret Psalm 110:1—"The LORD says to my Lord: 'Sit at my right hand...'"—as referring to Jesus' exaltation (Acts 2:34–35). Such appropriation of a Yahweh text for Jesus underscores that the apostles identified Him with Israel's God at a profound level (Hurtado, *Lord Jesus Christ*, 2003).

Paul's Transformation and Early Preaching

Another towering figure in early Christian testimony is **Paul the**

65

Apostle, originally a zealous Pharisee known as Saul of Tarsus. According to Acts 9:1–19, he encountered the risen Christ on the road to Damascus, an event that radically reshaped his theology and mission. Paul's own letters—among the earliest Christian writings we possess—reflect a consistent presentation of Jesus as both **Messiah** and **Lord**.

In passages such as **Philippians 2:6–11**, Paul cites an early Christian hymn that portrays Jesus as existing "in the form of God," yet humbling Himself to death on a cross before God exalts Him and bestows upon Him "the name that is above every name." Scholars note that this "name above every name" likely alludes to God's revealed name (YHWH), indicating the conferral of **divine honor** upon Jesus. The climax of this hymn—"every knee should bow... and every tongue confess that Jesus Christ is Lord"—echoes Isaiah 45:23, where Yahweh declares that every knee will bow to Him. Thus, in early Christian worship, language and imagery originally reserved for God alone are being applied to Jesus (Fee, *Paul's Letter to the Philippians*, 1995).

Paul further develops the concept of Jesus as **"Son of God"** in Romans 1:3–4, presenting Jesus' resurrection as proof that He is God's Son in power. While "Son of God" can in some biblical contexts refer to Israel's king or a righteous person, Paul's usage here and elsewhere in his epistles implies a **unique** filial relationship with the Father that transcends typical Jewish idioms. For Paul, faith in Jesus is tantamount to acknowledging His **divine lordship**, making the confession "Jesus is Lord" a central hallmark of Christian identity (Romans 10:9).

Apostolic Unity on Christ's Identity

Despite the diverse cultural contexts of Peter, Paul, James, John, and others, the **apostolic message** displays remarkable unity concerning Jesus' status. The Book of Acts (4:12) famously declares that "there is no other name under heaven given among men by which we must be saved." In 1 John 5:20, the Elder refers to Jesus Christ as the "true God and eternal life." The epistle to the Hebrews depicts Jesus as the **radiance of God's glory** and superior to angels (Hebrews 1:3–4). These texts exhibit a **variety of expressions**—Son of God, Lord, Image of God's glory, Christ, Messiah—yet converge on the notion that Jesus shares in God's unique identity.

Apostolic witness also often ties Jesus' divinity to practical ethics and community life. For example, 1 Corinthians 8:6 modifies the Shema, affirming "one God, the Father... and one Lord, Jesus Christ," setting Jesus alongside the Father in defining the identity of the one God. This daring reformulation of Israel's central confession demonstrates that from an early stage, Christians folded Jesus into **monotheistic** devotion. They did not see themselves as worshiping a second god but rather **recognizing** that the Father's identity was inseparable from His Son.

7.2 Worship of Jesus

Hymns, Prayers, and Liturgical Practices

One of the most striking pieces of evidence that the earliest believers regarded Jesus as divine is their **worship** of Him, which the New Testament describes in hymns, prayers, and doxologies. Beyond the Pauline hymn in Philippians 2, another crucial text is **Colossians 1:15–20**, often identified as a Christological hymn. It extols Jesus as "the image of the invisible God" and the one "in whom all things hold together." This language transcends that of a typical human figure, portraying Jesus as the **cosmic sustainer**—a role ascribed to God alone in Jewish tradition.

Additionally, in 1 Corinthians 16:22, believers exclaim **"Maranatha!"** ("Our Lord, come!"), an Aramaic prayer directed **to** Jesus. Early Christian gatherings appear to have included direct addresses to Jesus—petitions for His return and His help. This practice is significant because, in Judaism, **prayer** was customarily offered to God alone (cf. Nehemiah 2:4–5, 2 Chronicles 6:14–42). Thus, the presence of prayers to Jesus in Christian liturgy represents a **radical innovation** that signaled Jesus' inclusion within the divine identity (Bauckham, *Jesus and the God of Israel*, 2008).

Baptism in the Name of the Father, Son, and Holy Spirit

Another important liturgical development is the Trinitarian **baptismal formula**, exemplified in Matthew 28:19: "baptizing them in the name of the Father and of the Son and of the Holy Spirit." While the Book of Acts sometimes mentions baptizing in Jesus' name (Acts 2:38), these variations suggest that the earliest church understood **baptism** as an initiation into a relationship with both **God the Father** and **Jesus** (and subsequently the Holy Spirit). The merging of Jesus' name with the Father's name is another clear indication that the Church, from its formative years, treated Jesus as **co-equal** in identity with God.

Historically, Jewish mikvah (ritual immersion) was a cleansing rite, whereas Christian baptism took on a **Christ-centered** orientation. Converts declared allegiance to Jesus as Lord, trusting in Him for salvation. Even if the theology of the Trinity was not fully articulated at this early stage, the baptismal practice implied an integral **tie** between Jesus and the one God of Israel. Over time, as the Church reflected on these practices, doctrines about **Jesus' divinity** became more explicit in creeds and catechetical instructions, but the seeds of that doctrine were sown from the moment the first believers began to baptize in His name.

Eucharist and Confessing Christ

The **Eucharist** (or Lord's Supper) also had profound Christological implications. Early Christians broke bread and shared the cup "in remembrance" of Jesus (Luke 22:19–20, 1 Corinthians 11:24–26). In Paul's theology, the Eucharist not only memorialized Jesus' sacrificial death but also fostered **communion** with the risen Christ

(1 Corinthians 10:16–17). The notion that believers participated in "the body and blood" of Jesus resonates with a high Christology, wherein the crucified and risen One is understood to be **spiritually present** and intimately involved in the life of His church.

By the late first century and early second century, Christian worship texts (e.g., the **Didache**) reveal that prayers and blessings were directed explicitly to Jesus in the context of the Eucharistic meal. While the Didache does not present a fully developed theological system, it does evidence a community that treats Jesus as **the authoritative Lord,** deserving of thanksgiving and praise typically reserved for God. Hence, worshiping Jesus through Word, prayer, and sacramental rites was **already** a central feature of the earliest church's identity.

7.3 Expansion of Early Christianity

The Rapid Spread Throughout the Mediterranean

Historians note that **Christianity** grew with striking speed across the Roman Empire, reaching major urban centers such as Antioch, Corinth, and Rome within a few decades of Jesus' death and resurrection. Sociologically, Rodney Stark's studies suggest that the Christian movement expanded from a small group of perhaps a few hundred believers to several million by the fourth century (Stark, *The Rise of Christianity*, 1996). Central to this growth was the **proclamation** that in Jesus, the one God of Israel had decisively acted to redeem all people—Jews and Gentiles alike.

Christian missionaries, like Paul, Barnabas, and others, traveled extensively, **planting communities** that met in homes. These communities rapidly developed their own leadership structures— elders, overseers (bishops), and deacons—but held in common the confession of Jesus' lordship and divinity. As Gentile converts came to faith, they often left behind polytheistic worship practices and embraced the exclusive worship of Jesus alongside the Father. The theological shock of worshiping a crucified Jew as **"Lord"** was significant, yet many found in this new faith a compelling combination of **moral transformation, social equality** (Galatians 3:28), and **spiritual power**.

Why Belief in Jesus' Deity Spread

One might question how such a **monumental claim**—that a Jewish man from a small province of the Roman Empire was actually God incarnate—could have spread so widely. Several factors contributed to this phenomenon:

1. **Resurrection Proclamation:** The earliest apostolic preaching centered on **Jesus' resurrection** as a historical event (1 Corinthians 15:3–8). For audiences aware of Jewish beliefs in a coming age of resurrection, the claim that God had already raised one man signaled a **new eschatological reality**. If Jesus was risen and reigning, it implied His exalted, divine status.

2. **Spiritual Experiences:** Early communities reported manifestations of the **Holy Spirit**—healings, prophetic utterances, speaking in tongues (Acts 2, 1 Corinthians 12–14). These supernatural experiences reinforced the claim that Jesus was present and active among them, validating apostolic testimony.

3. **Ethical and Relational Transformation:** Christianity offered a distinctive vision of **love, forgiveness**, and **communal care** (Acts 2:44–47). Converts from various social strata found a new sense of belonging that overcame ethnic and class barriers. Such a radical ethic was seen as emanating from Jesus' own divine authority and example.

4. **Martyrdom and Conviction:** Many Christians, including the apostles, were willing to **face persecution and death** rather than renounce Jesus. Notable examples include Stephen (Acts 7), James (Acts 12:2), and tradition holds that most apostles met martyrdom for their faith. Their

70

willingness to die for their belief in Jesus' divinity lent credibility and moral force to their message.

Thus, the idea that Jesus was "God among us" was not a mere philosophical proposition but a lived reality for communities that testified to personal transformation, miraculous interventions, and a profound **unity** that crossed traditional boundaries. Over time, Christian thinkers like Justin Martyr, Irenaeus, and Tertullian would articulate more formal **apologies** (defenses of the faith) to Roman authorities and intellectuals, explaining why Jesus deserved the same reverence as the God worshiped in Judaism (Justin Martyr, *First Apology*, c. AD 155).

The Role of the Holy Spirit in the Church's Witness

Central to early Christian self-understanding was the conviction that the **Holy Spirit** guided their **proclamation** and **community life** (John 14:16–17; Acts 1:8). From Pentecost onward, the Spirit was believed to empower believers for mission, embolden them to preach, and confirm the message with signs. This divine empowerment played a vital role in overcoming barriers of language and culture, as well as providing the **internal conviction** that Jesus' status as Lord was not merely an idea but a spiritual reality affirmed by God Himself.

Over time, the recognition of the Spirit's work, combined with the already established confession of the Father and the Son, contributed to what would eventually develop into **Trinitarian theology**. The earliest believers may not have had a formalized doctrine of the Trinity, but they consistently spoke of the Father, Son, and Spirit in ways that assumed **unity of essence** and **distinction of persons**. While the complex theological formulations would come later (at councils such as Nicaea in AD 325 and Chalcedon in AD 451), the seeds were present in the daily worship, prayers, and experiences of the first-generation churches.

Concluding Thoughts

From its earliest days, the **Christian community** collectively bore witness to Jesus as **God incarnate**—a conviction displayed through apostolic preaching, communal worship, and bold missionary outreach. Key figures like **Peter** and **Paul** staked their entire message on Jesus' identity as both Israel's Messiah and the divine Lord exalted to God's right hand. Their sermons and letters reveal that the earliest believers did not view Jesus merely as a revered teacher but as sharing in the **name, power, and worship** reserved for Yahweh.

The formation of **Christian worship** practices—particularly in hymnody, prayers, baptism, and the Eucharist—centered on reverence for Jesus as divine. Congregations prayed **to** Jesus, praised Him in doxologies, and baptized converts in His name alongside the Father's, forging a liturgical identity that placed Jesus at the very heart of monotheistic devotion. This was a radical shift in a Jewish milieu that worshiped one God, as well as in a Greco-Roman world accustomed to many gods.

Finally, the astonishing **expansion** of Christianity throughout the Mediterranean basin and beyond was largely propelled by the unwavering belief that Jesus is "Lord." Converts from Judaism, paganism, and other backgrounds embraced the claim that God had revealed Himself uniquely in Jesus, whose resurrection overcame death and whose Spirit empowered the Church. Despite persecution, misunderstanding, and internal disputes over how best to articulate these truths, the **central testimony** remained consistent: Jesus Christ is worthy of worship, and in Him, the God of Israel is present and active in a new, definitive way.

This early Christian witness set the stage for the theological controversies and councils of later centuries, yet from the very beginning, the Church's core was marked by the bold proclamation that the crucified and risen Jesus is, indeed, **God with us**.

Chapter 8: Conclusion- Looking Beyond the Question

8.1 Revisiting the Central Question

The inquiry "Is Jesus God?" has guided this entire book, driving an extensive examination of biblical texts, historical developments, and theological concepts. Throughout these pages, we have explored how Jesus' words, actions, and the testimony of early Christians consistently point toward a reality that goes beyond ordinary human categories. Yet even after sifting through scriptural evidence, early church testimonies, and doctrinal reflections, the question remains a **matter of faith**.

In one sense, this concluding chapter affirms the central theme: traditional Christian teaching maintains that in Jesus, God has revealed Himself fully—He is not merely a gifted teacher or a moral exemplar, but the **incarnate** divine Son. However, the significance of this claim rests not only in textual and historical analysis but also in its **transformational potential**. To believe that Jesus is God means to enter a story in which the Creator takes on human form, shares humanity's sufferings, and overcomes the ultimate barrier of death—forever bridging the chasm between finite creatures and the infinite Divine.

The Inescapability of Interpretation

Despite carefully marshaled evidence and centuries of theological reflection, the question "Is Jesus God?" remains inescapably tied to **interpretation**. One's worldview, cultural background, and personal experiences shape how one encounters the figure of Jesus. While Christian communities affirm that this is not simply a subjective matter—pointing to creedal confessions and scriptural testimony—reading these texts or encountering Christian worship with an open mind still involves **human perception**. As the writer of Hebrews notes, "Without faith it is impossible to please God" (Hebrews 11:6), indicating that pure rationality alone does not fully capture the essence of confessing Jesus' deity.

8.2 Reflecting on the Evidence: Beyond Historical and Literary Analysis

Having traversed biblical scholarship, church history, and theological discussions, this book has weighed various strands of **evidence**. Yet historical inquiry, textual criticism, and doctrinal statements only take us so far in confronting the claim that Jesus is God.

The Role of Personal Encounter

Among the earliest Christians, **personal encounter** played a pivotal role in shaping their belief that Jesus was divine. Many testified to meeting the risen Christ, experiencing miracles, or receiving the Holy Spirit in a dramatic way. While modern readers may not share identical experiences, personal or communal encounters still shape the contemporary journey toward embracing Jesus as God. Such encounters might be found in **prayer, worship**, acts of **service**, or in moments of deep struggle or awe that reveal a presence beyond human explanation.

Comparative religion scholars note that few world faiths center so explicitly on God's embodiment in a specific historical person. Islam reveres Muhammad as a prophet but does not claim he is God. Buddhism does not identify Siddhartha Gautama as a deity, and Judaism rejects the notion of God becoming flesh in Jesus. But in Christianity, incarnation marks a **unique** dimension, inviting believers to see creation itself as capable of carrying the divine. The question "Is Jesus God?" here transcends a purely historical proposition that affirms God's radical closeness to humanity.

Significance in a Postmodern Context

In a **postmodern** cultural context where absolute truth claims can be met with skepticism, the assertion that "Jesus is God" challenges prevailing pluralisms and relativisms. Some argue that all religious claims are equally valid (or equally uncertain). In Christianity, God became fully human in Jesus stands as a decisive, particular truth factor.

8.3 Implications for Faith and Practice

Worship and Spiritual Devotion

For those who affirm Jesus as God, **worship** takes on a distinct character. If Jesus is indeed one with the Creator, then adoration directed toward Him is not idolatry but proper reverence. Hymns, prayers, and sacraments that honor Jesus as Lord become central acts of **communion** with God. Within many Christian traditions, the Eucharist or Lord's Supper is seen as a tangible expression of Christ's presence—feeding believers not merely with a symbol but with the living reality of the divine-human Savior.

Furthermore, personal **devotional** practices—such as meditation on the Gospels, contemplative prayer, or reading spiritual classics—often revolve around Jesus' divine identity. Believers seek to encounter Jesus not as a distant historical figure but as the **ever-present Word** who speaks into their daily life. Liturgical calendars, feast days (e.g., Christmas, Easter), and other ecclesial rhythms underscore this reality, reminding worshippers that they inhabit a story where the divine and the human have fused in Christ.

Ethics and Mission

A belief in Jesus' deity also shapes **ethical** perspectives. If God in Christ has walked among humans, cared for the marginalized, washed His disciples' feet, and offered Himself in sacrificial love, then the Christian moral life must mirror this **self-giving** ethos. The standard is no less than the character of God as revealed in Jesus. Consequently, Christian communities historically have championed care for the sick, the poor, and the oppressed, seeing in such acts the **continuation** of Jesus' work in the world (Matthew 25:40).

Mission and evangelism likewise find their grounding here. The impetus to **spread the gospel**—telling others that Jesus is Lord—is not a mere sectarian impulse but a response to the conviction that humanity's Creator has revealed Himself in a once-for-all event. If Jesus is truly God, then inviting others into relationship with Him becomes an urgent priority, not simply another philosophical conversation. This divine-human dynamic fuels Christian mission, making it more than ethical activism; it is a shared spiritual journey toward the One who unites humanity with divinity.

8.4 Ecumenical and Interfaith Perspectives

Ecumenical Christian Dialogue

The question "Is Jesus God?" has, ironically, been a **unifying** and **dividing** factor within the broader Christian tradition. While all mainstream Christian denominations—Catholic, Orthodox, Protestant—affirm Jesus' divinity, how exactly His divine and human natures coexist has sparked centuries of theological debate. From the early councils of Nicaea (AD 325) and Chalcedon (AD 451) to modern ecumenical dialogues, Christological controversies have shaped the boundaries of **orthodoxy**.

In contemporary contexts, ecumenical efforts often focus on bridging secondary disagreements to present a **united witness** to Christ's deity. Churches that once feuded over nuances of Christ's person can now find common ground in worshiping Jesus as the incarnate Word, reflecting a shared historical creed that He is "God from God, Light from Light, true God from true God" (Nicene Creed). This ecumenical spirit underscores that affirming Jesus as God is a fundamental, unifying confession across the Christian world, even if practice and liturgical forms vary widely.

8.5 A Final Invitation: Embracing with Hope

The Continuing Journey of Discovery

Concluding this book entitled "Is Jesus God? - God in the Flesh: Jesus' Divine Identity" does not mean the conversation has ended. If anything, affirming Jesus' deity opens vast horizons of theological exploration and personal devotion. The incarnational claim that "the Word became flesh" (John 1:14) implies that every dimension of human existence—work, relationships, suffering, joy—can be permeated by divine grace. Discipleship, then, is not limited to intellectual assent; it is an ongoing encounter with Christ in prayer, community life, and service.

Readers who have journeyed through these chapters, weighing the evidence and examining the testimonies, may stand at different vantage points. Some may find themselves **convinced**, ready to affirm that Jesus is indeed God incarnate, while others may still harbor doubts or seek further clarity. Still others may approach from a non-Christian background, wanting to understand why Christians hold this belief so tenaciously. Regardless of one's position, to understand the question of Jesus' identity, I challenge you to embrace with hope and faith to taste and see that He is the Lord and God.

Hope in the Face of Mystery

Calling Jesus "God" does not dissolve all mysteries. Indeed, it can intensify them. How can God be both transcendent and immanent, both infinite and yet incarnate in a first-century Jewish man? How does the eternal Word experience pain, death, and resurrection? The **paradox** of Jesus' two natures—human and divine—continues to prompt awe and reflection. Historically, Christian theology has held that certain aspects of God's nature will remain incomprehensible to finite minds, even as the Incarnation assures us that God's love is intimately accessible.

This paradox fosters **hope**. If Jesus is God, then **love, compassion**, and **mercy** are not mere human constructs but derive from the very heart of the Creator. Suffering and injustice, though profound, do not have the final word—because the same God who entered suffering overcame it in resurrection. For believers, therefore, the claim that Jesus is God becomes the foundation for an **abiding hope** that the brokenness of the world can be healed, that sin can be forgiven, and that death can be conquered.

Stepping Beyond the Final Page

As we close this book, we acknowledge that **faith** does not rest on a single argument, nor is it arrived at solely by reading. It requires a personal, communal, and existential embrace. For those inclined to take the next step, the journey might involve **prayerful reflection**, joining a Christian community, or conversing with spiritual mentors who have walked this path before. For skeptics or seekers, continued dialogue with other viewpoints can bring deeper understanding, even if one remains uncertain.

Ultimately, the question "Is Jesus God?" leads us to call Jesus "Lord and God" (John 20:28) is to stand at the threshold of a transformative relationship. May this book serve as a door opener to that relationship—or at least a vantage point from which its contours become more visible.

www.ingramcontent.com/pod-product-compliance
Lightning Source LLC
Chambersburg PA
CBHW060349050426
42449CB00011B/2897